RESEARCHER

The Power and Potential of Research Careers for Women

Women in Academia Support Network (WIASN)

United Kingdom – North America – Japan – India
Malaysia – China

Emerald Publishing Limited
Howard House, Wagon Lane, Bingley BD16 1WA, UK

First edition 2022

Reprints and permissions service
Contact: permissions@emeraldinsight.com

British Library Cataloguing in Publication Data
A catalogue record for this book is available from the British
Library

ISBN: 978-1-80382-734-6 (Print)
ISBN: 978-1-80382-731-5 (Online)
ISBN: 978-1-80382-733-9 (Epub)

ISOQAR certified
Management System,
awarded to Emerald
for adherence to
Environmental
standard
ISO 14001:2004.

Certificate Number 1985
ISO 14001

INVESTOR IN PEOPLE

CONTENTS

ACKNOWLEDGEMENTS

The WIASN team are:

Dr Amy Bonsall: Founder, Director and Editor of this book.

Dr Kelly Pickard-Smith: Co-founder, Director and Editor of this book.

Prof. Eleonora Belfiore: Co-founder, Director and Editor of this book.

Dr Maxine Horne: Co-founder and Director.

Catherine Beard: Co-founders and Director.

To the most important people – our children. We aren't sure how much you helped or hindered the book production process with demands for more juice and biscuits, the bouts of Covid and inevitable home-schooling during a global pandemic but the cuddles, the hugs, the fun and the laughter always get us through the difficult times and we know the work we do is to benefit you and the generations that come behind us.

This book wouldn't be possible without the care and support of all of the women in the WIASN network and this includes special mention to our moderators Nia Wearn and Peny Sotiropoulou, and to all the academics voluntarily running our 20+ special interest groups on topics such as mental health, working-class academics, academics on the move, beyond cancer, ECRs and writing support, to name just a few. Our members give their time with care and compassion and also keep each other in check with regard to our many

privileges. We thank each and every one for the humbling opportunity to showcase just a small part of the work that you do. Having you in research careers makes all our lives richer.

To our publishers Emerald Publishing. Emerald have been supporters of WIASN from our conception. They have a commitment to gender equity in research and really do put their money where their mouth is. When we came to them and said we want to produce a book in less than six months they said let's make this happen. Despite this book not being the usual academic publication. Their dedication to gender equity and the support they gave with the illustrations and marketing means so much to us, long may this partnership continue.

We were very grateful to be one of the 131 global communities, and one of only 10 from the UK (from over 40,000 applications) to have received Facebook Community Accelerator funding that enabled us to produce an initial print fund of 1,000 books to be distributed to 1,000 schools for free to reach a potential 1 million students through their school libraries.

Finally, with a fundraiser we hope to get more free books into more schools. If you contributed to the fundraiser or bought the book as a gift know you are also contributing to gifting this book to communities who are systematically blocked from participating in higher education and research and you have contributed to breaking down those barriers – even in some small way.

Thank you.

INTRODUCTION – WOMEN IN ACADEMIA SUPPORT NETWORK – WHO EVEN ARE WE AND WHAT DO WE DO?

Women in Academia Support Network (WIASN) began in 2017 when a group of strangers digitally met on an academic Facebook group for early career academics. Through engaging in that space it became obvious that there were very few platforms for female identifying academics to come together to network, learn and share experiences.

WIASN is a trans-inclusive, intersectional network for women and all people who have lived experience of misogyny in their role as academics.

These strangers (now colleagues and best friends) started the Facebook community group "WIASN' (pronounced Wise-un) with a vision that access to higher education and research can be changed from a grass roots collective and a mission to take the power and make radical action now! Shaping higher education and research from within – through online community activism.

Improving routes into higher education and research for women and then retaining those women was really important because society benefits from the expertise of diverse people. Unfortunately, it is still the case that careers in higher education and research are difficult to obtain and retain because of

stereotypes about who does research and what research is and keeping people out because of their gender, sexuality, race, religion and class. Only 1% of the global population have a Philosophy Doctorate (PhD) and more than half of those PhDs awarded are to women. Yet women remain more likely to be pushed out their careers after PhD and are woefully underrepresented in senior roles. We need women to stay in research and to excel because gender diversity benefits everyone through diverse perspectives.

WIASN now have over 12,000 members, from PhD to Vice Chancellor, in over 100 countries and different research sectors (because not all research happens in labs or in universities). Our aim is to encourage and keep women in research careers through the use of mutual support networks and advocacy/activism. We hope, through this book, that more women will embark on and remain in research careers.

Before we formally introduce ourselves as researchers and as the book editors we have a task for you. We want you to do some drawing. It's a simple instruction:

Draw a Scientist.

Finished? Now turn the page...

WHAT EVEN IS RESEARCH?

You've just participated in a famous research study called the Draw a Scientist Test (DAST). It was developed by David Wade Chamber in 1983 who wanted to find out when we started stereotyping what a scientist is and looks like. In the original research nearly 5,000 primary school children in three countries were asked to draw a scientist. Most of the drawings were pictures of white men in labs wearing white coats and glasses. While over the years the number of women drawn in the test has increased there is still a lack of representation in other ways such as disability, and the lab coat and glasses seem to remain. This study tells us that scientists are usually men, usually white, able bodied and that science (and therefore research) takes place in a lab.

But you've just participated in some science with your drawing. So we already know that not all science takes place in a lab and also not all science is about experiments and people in white coats.

This is where the book *ResearcHER* comes in. We wanted to smash stereotypes of not only who does research but also what research is. You can research an infinite number of things in so many different ways. Take the Editors of this book, for example:

Dr Kelly Pickard-Smith: Kelly grew up in Wythenshawe, once of the most deprived areas in the UK. Kelly came to higher education as an adult through a six-year distance degree with the Open University sitting her final exams at 32 years old and two weeks before her first son was born. Two years later there was another baby and she studied her MA with two children under two years while working as a tutor to support disadvantaged young people into education and employment. Her PhD came soon after and she won a scholarship to the University of Manchester where she used improvisational drama

and film to explore people's experiences of mathematics education to understand inequality in mathematically demanding careers such as science. Then baby 3 arrived. Kelly is also disabled with chronic long-term illness (heart arrhythmia and pernicious anaemia) and an obsessive compulsive disorder plus as yet not professionally diagnosed probable attention deficit hyperactivity disorder (ADHD). She is a strong advocate against disability discrimination.

Dr Amy Bonsall: Amy has researched how Shakespeare had been adapted in the African country of Malawi, working with local professional actors to put on a performance of Romeo ndi Julieti (Romeo and Juliet) translated in to Chichewa by renowned Malawian writer Stanley Onjezani Kenani and then adapted for performance by Amy and Misheck Mzumara. Amy is dyslexic and has obsessive compulsive disorder (OCD) and achieving her PhD was a huge highlight for her, especially as she was not invited back to high school to do A-level as they said she didn't understand Shakespeare! Amy has won awards for her work on disability advocacy in higher education and research. Amy founded WIASN. As an international theatre director, Amy works with professional companies to bring theatre to life for public audiences.

Professor Eleonora Belfiore: Eleonora researches cultural politics and policy and the social impact of the arts on British culture and politics. Eleonora is internationally renowned in her field and is the Journal Editor for Cultural Trends. A Sicilian living in the UK, Eleonora has brought a unique perspective to the cultural sector and UK cultural arts policy and has received prestigious Arts and Humanities Research Council (AHRC) research council funding to explore everyday participation and the connecting of communities through arts and culture. Eleonora is also a strong disability rights advocate sharing her lived experience of the process of ADHD diagnosis, since there is an under diagnosing of ADHD in women given

how differently symptoms can be displayed compared to the more widely understood male presentation.

As you can see from our short bios, there is diversity in research if we scratch the surface in respect of what is researched and who is doing the research. We developed the *ResearcHER* book to showcase amazing women researchers doing varied types of research to highlight that science and research doesn't just happen in a lab (it sometimes does) and that what can be researched is infinite. Through the book we explore vignettes (short stories and bios) of 28 fabulous researchers from different backgrounds, countries and research fields to get a sense of the importance of diverse voices in research and also to give some examples of short activities you can do to try out some research techniques of your own.

Because of diversity in research careers, researchers may also have different titles. Titles include: Dr (Doctor), Professor, Associate Professor, Lecturer, Senior Lecturer, Reader, Research Associate, Research Fellow and Independent Researcher – all are Researchers but not all will be Doctors/Dr.

Undertaking and passing a PhD entitles you to use to title Doctor/Dr but it is different to a medical doctorate (MD) – although some medics also have PhDs! Confused yet? A PhD is an intensive period of study where you create a research question then design how you will go about researching it and then analyse your results. As part of the research you usually produce a large written piece of work detailing the research question, literature about your topic, the methods you used, the data/information you collected, how you analysed that data and then what you found out – your results. This piece of written work is usually 70,000–100,000 words long and is called a thesis. But some PhD theses can be much shorter; for example, if you included science experiments or did a practice-based (Education or arts/performance, e.g.) PhD. When you finish your PhD you have to 'defend' it. In

many countries this is called a viva voce, where you have to speak to senior academics (researchers) who will question you about the research. In some countries, like Finland, you are even given a sword to hold during your 'defence'! The Dr title is awarded as a note to your educational achievement and only passing this process allows you to use that title. All other titles are professional so Professor, for example, is bestowed by whichever university hires you through their selection or promotion process and if you leave or retire you do not necessarily take that title with you.

However, not all researchers or lecturer are Doctors because industry and experience are also routes into higher education lecturing and research careers. Also, not all research careers happen in universities. Researchers work in many varied industries and sectors, such as health care, pharmaceuticals, aerospace, charities, government and even Facebook and Amazon have researchers. Research careers are, therefore, very varied.

A quick note on titles. Using the correct title for women researchers is very important. Women are more often introduced without their Dr or Professor title then men. However, to accommodate all these varied research careers and so you can get to know the researchers in a more informal way we won't be using titles like Dr or Prof. in the book unless the author has included it in their biography.

Finally, and most importantly, we must acknowledge that research remains biased to Western higher education and is heavily dominated by white male academics. While this book is to address gender equity in research and showcase amazing women researchers we need to point out that where there has been some progress in gender equity, it is mostly white women, able bodied, *cis*-gendered and heterosexual women who have benefitted and much, much more needs to be done to diversify women in higher education and research.

Research needs to be diverse because diversity of thought will help solve some of the world's most pressing problems and, importantly, innovate and be creative. In this book, you will find ResearcHERs who have written about their backgrounds, why they got into research and the types of varied research they do. They have even provided some small activities you can get involved with to encourage you to start thinking about science and research in different ways. We hope you enjoy the book. We really enjoyed working with so many different and fabulous women.

So come and draw your research, dance it, perform it, sing it, film it, interview for it, do an experiment for it, do it on the stage, in the supermarket, in a school, in the street, in space, out at sea, in a lab. Research whatever and wherever but come be a

ResearcHER

FATIMA A. JUNAID

Age: 45
Ethnicity: I am a Pashtun Muslim. I am from Pakistan, Asia
Gender and sexuality: She/her. Woman, Female, straight
Geographical location: Manawatu, New Zealand
Current institution: Massey University, New Zealand

ABOUT ME

Mother, Woman, Muslim, Wife, Daughter, Researcher, Sister, Friend, Brown, Academic, Relative, Nature lover, Pakistani, Mentor, Asian. (Perhaps in that order.)

I am a brown woman, from Pakistan's most conservative province. I come from the tribal side of the Khyber Pakhtoon Khawa Province (KPK). I am a practicing Muslim, who is married out of her sect (Shia Muslim married to Sunni Muslim). I have two daughters; aged 15 and three years.

My education has been a means of my liberty. I fought for five years to marry the person of my choice, whom I love and who supports me and my educational journey. Where I come from, it is very hard (if not impossible) to make it without the support of the male members of your house. With his support, I have stood up against institutional injustices. I also acknowledge the support of my family, my mother, sisters and brother, in helping me stay sane.

After coming to New Zealand, in the first year of my PhD, which is on 'job stress and PTSD due to terrorism, and its

9

influence on employee behaviours', I lost my father in a bomb blast in a mosque. With the help of my supervisors and family, and by the Grace of Allah, I finished it in four years.

I am the only woman in both my own and my husband's family with a PhD. I speak Pashto, Urdu and English. I have read the translation of the Quran numerous times.

Inspired by Women in Academia Support Network (WIASN) I started a closed safe group for 'Pakistani women in Academia' to support women who want to pursue research and academia.

I have a love for learning and sharing the learnings, it has helped me expand my thinking in understanding how people from different backgrounds think.

FUN FACT

As a kid I use to find it fascinating to look at ants move on grass blades, I would lie down on the grass and watch them do their chores for hours (sometimes I wonder if parents of today's time had seen me, they would feel concerned?)

When I go to flower gardens, I smell almost every flower. I feed and watch the birds for hours. I think standing under big trees is a joy.

MY RESEARCH

Anything I research relates eventually with 'wellbeing'. Within organisational behaviour and psychology, I am interested in stress, trauma, grief, gratitude, psychosocial risks at work, organisational support and psychological capital. I am also interested in studying marginalised people in general and women specifically and their wellbeing.

My current research looks at exclusion of women in Pakistani academic spaces. The study uses vignettes based on our

personal experiences, but slightly broadened and anonymised. Women academics are asked to share their stories of exclusion especially focusing on physical space. The data is collected through Facebook.

One of our recent studies is looking at refugee women wellbeing and their entrepreneurship journeys in New Zealand. Another study is on working women wellbeing in Pakistan, which covers the hardships, exclusion and other psychosocial risks at work. We will hear difficult stories, but those voices need to be heard and known. Hopefully, these studies will provide narratives of resilience, which will give hope to others.

I became a researcher because I was always curious about things. Reading the 'Tell Me Why?' book series was my favourite hobby. While I lived in Pakistan, a student of mine once got 90% burnt when a suicide bomber blasted himself at an eatery where large numbers of male students used to eat. It was an open cooking area, and the suicide bomber was near the gas cylinder which was used in the open cooking area. My student was standing next to it.

His entire class was shocked, and we all cried and prayed for his life. Miraculously he survived and is well. That day I started thinking – 'what are the impacts of living under ongoing terrorism on (us) those living in Pakistan and how it affected our behaviours at work?' – that became my PhD.

My PhD made me realise that I am interested in 'wellbeing'.

FUN FACT

Many times, people think that my research area is sad. In reality, it is a positive. If I study grief, burnout, anxiety, post-traumatic stress disorder, exclusion or stress, it eventually leads to how support in different contexts can help better it.

ACTIVITY

I recently completed a study on Health and Safety Representatives using the 'World Café' method to collect data regarding lessons learnt in COVID-19. World Café method allowed participants to respond as a group sitting on a table (like a café). Then they go to other tables and chat with others about it, similar to a chat we have with someone in a café. Finally, they come back to their original tables and as a group write collectively as they share their learnings with one another. It was appreciated because the participants felt that they not only gave us data but also learnt from each other.

Sharing stories are powerful and ancient ways of learning about the world. Think about how sitting on a table like a café can make sharing stories and experiences easier to tell and share. Find an opportunity to sit with friends, people you study with or work with and how, through sitting together and talking you are learning about how you experienced the COVID-19 pandemic or any other significant life events from each other.

JENNIFER A. RUDD

Age: 34
Ethnicity: White
Gender and sexuality: Female, straight
Geographical location: Wales, UK
Current institution: Swansea University, UK

ABOUT ME

People have always called me weird! I went through school as the 'nerd' with my head in a book, not understanding social interactions, speaking very bluntly, and seeing things differently to everyone else. It's taken until the age of 34 to realise that I'm not 'weird', I'm autistic! I act differently and think differently because my brain is wired differently to everyone else's. I'm still in the early stages of discovering more about how I can work best and how I can help my colleagues accept me just the way I am. I've been getting support from a lot of different places, and it is all helping me to finally be me, rather than someone I think I should be.

I'm also a female who has worked in chemistry and engineering departments in four different countries. When I walked into the chemistry lab in America for the first-time people stopped and said 'oh my gosh you're a woman'. I remember looking down and thinking 'well yes, is this going to be a problem?'. I've also had comments like 'you can't work late/move abroad you have a family'.

When I worked in engineering, I worked in a university campus known as the 'boy's campus'. I couldn't believe how many men there were everywhere! However, there, I was fortunate to work in a team who didn't care about my gender. If I did good work and was a team player then I was accepted and respected.

FUN FACT

Despite the fact that I'm a passionate advocate for decreasing the world's carbon footprint, I used to be an air cadet. I've flown small planes and I've been in three different types of helicopters!

MY RESEARCH

I research climate change education. I want to answer the question 'Can we teach climate change in a way that effects behavioural change'. I get to work with three amazing women, specialists in psychology, education and creative writing/digital skills. We created You and CO_2, which is a programme of climate change education for secondary schools that empowers students to act on climate change, rather than just learn about it. In addition, I collaborate with people in different education settings in Wales, the UK and abroad, to develop new climate change curricula.

I grew up learning that fossil fuels were running out. I did a chemistry degree at the University of York, then a PhD in chemistry in Switzerland. While studying, I spent all my time thinking about making solar panels for when fossil fuels ran out. Then, in 2018, I learnt about climate change and the devastating effects it would have on our planet. I changed my whole research field, from chemistry and engineering to climate change education in response. I wanted other people

to know about climate change and how to fix it. I wanted to use my ability to read and summarise complicated science reports so that the information was accessible to other people. I want young people to grow up feeling empowered to act on climate change and not make the same mistakes that generations have made before us. I want to see system change not climate change.

FUN FACT

I want to use my research to read people's minds!

With You and CO_2 we want to know whether we can teach teenagers about climate change in a way that makes them change their attitudes and behaviours. We are collecting data in words, numbers and computer mouse clicks. When we put all these together, we are hoping we can build up a picture of how that teenager thinks climate change can be solved and whether participating in our programme has changed their thoughts or actions with respect to climate change.

ACTIVITY

As part of the You and CO_2 project we have an online story. It's set in Metra, a moon colony, which is dependent on earth for raw materials, food and communications. You join the story just before communications with earth end unexpectedly. Your job is to figure out why that has happened.

The story has multiple endings depending on decisions you make as you read through. You can personalise it with your name and friends' names and gender pronouns. See if you can find all six endings! You can find the You and CO_2 project activity by putting this link into your web browser if you have one: www.youandco2.org/NW4T.

As a paper activity think about what kinds or raw materials you would need from earth to be able to build your colony. What items would you need to house your colony, provide power, food, water, and sanitation? Draw, list or make a collage of the items/raw materials.

JENNY-LEE THOMASSIN

Age: 36
Ethnicity: Caucasian, Canadian (originally from the province of Québec)
Gender and sexuality: Female, woman, heterosexual. Married with children (child 1 b. 2014, child 2 b. 2015)
Geographical location: Saskatoon, Saskatchewan, Canada
Current institution: University of Saskatchewan, Canada

ABOUT ME

I grew up on the outskirts of Montreal in Quebec, Canada with three sisters and a brother. My father's family is of mixed French-Canadian and Ontarian heritage, and my mother's family emigrated to Canada from Ireland and England. I wouldn't say that there is anything remarkable about my childhood; I completed primary school in French before moving on to complete my secondary education in English. I completed a year of CEGEP, before moving to Halifax Nova Scotia for my Bachelor of sciences at Saint Mary's University. After three years, I completed my BSc with Honours in Biology and a Diploma in Forensic Sciences. At the end of my BSc, I had not yet secured an MSc position, so I worked for the regional residential services society until I found a position. I joined Dr. Nikhil Thomas' Group at Dalhousie University and completed my MSc thesis. I then moved back to Montreal where I completed my PhD under the supervision of

Dr Samantha Gruenheid and Dr Hervé Le Moual. I returned to Dr Le Moual's laboratory after my first maternity leave to complete a short postdoctoral fellowship. After a second maternity leave, I moved to Paris, France, where I worked as part of Dr. Olivera Francetic's Group at the Institute Pasteur, as part of a multidisciplinary group that combined structure and function to understand a bacterial nanomachine. I also worked with Dr Guy Tran Van Nhieu, at the Collège de France, where I learned and applied fluorescence microscopy techniques. I am now an Assistant Professor at the University of Saskatchewan.

FUN FACT

If I had not chosen to study biology, I would have studied history. I absolutely love learning how geography, culture, socioeconomics and global events have influenced historical events, cuisine and architecture. Luckily, my husband shares many of the same interests and on our first trip to Europe we were able to visit Nora, Italy. The ruins and mosaic tiles were beautiful. Since this first European trip, we were fortunate enough to move to France to complete our postdoctoral training, which allowed us to return to Europe to visit so many more historical sites and share the experience with our children.

MY RESEARCH

My research interests are focused on how bacteria interact with and shape their surrounding environment. This can be related to how bacteria survive in the environment, such as in waterways, or how they are able to grow in human or animal hosts. I am specifically focused on understanding the nuts and bolts, also called molecular mechanisms, involved in the

transport of molecules in and out of bacteria. I want to understand how these molecules allow bacteria to shape the world around them. The applications for my work are quite varied and range from simply understanding how things work to being able to provide chemists and other scientists with targets for the design of new smart drugs to treat bacterial infections.

When I started University, my goal was to become a forensic scientist. In my forensics courses, I loved collecting evidence and piecing it together. I also enjoyed other courses, including advanced plant sciences. Therefore, I completed an undergraduate honour's project in plant sciences. When working on this project, I was asked to collect a bacterial culture from a neighbouring laboratory and inoculate my plants with it. I did, and was amazed to see that the plant roots formed nodules and that they turned bright red. When I learned more about this process, I was amazed that the changes I had seen in the plant roots were driven by the bacteria as they worked to fix nitrogen, which is a critical process in our global nitrogen cycle. From this time onwards, I was hooked on bacteria and have focused on trying to understand how they interact with and shape their environment.

FUN FACT

Most of my time is spent doing the equivalent of arts and crafts with bacterial DNA. I take bits of DNA, cut them out and glue them back together slightly differently to see what

will happen. Planning these experiments and imagining what will happen to the bacterium as a result is one of the aspects of my work that I enjoy the most. The best part of this process is that most of the time what happens is much more interesting than I could ever imagine.

ACTIVITY

I often describe the work I do as trying to figure out how a tiny motor works, with the main challenge being that you are working in the dark, you cannot touch any of the individual pieces and your only output is often to determine whether the machine still works after you remove or modify a part of the machine.

A way to gain an understanding of the fun and frustration of this work is to play a game. You can ask a friend to build a machine using K'Nex or a gears motorized building set that turns a wheel at the end of a circuit. Then, you receive a list of all the possible parts used to build the machine, without an indication of how many of each piece was used or how they fit together. Then, without looking at the assembled machine, you ask your friend to remove a specific piece of the machine. For example, remove the red pieces that are 3-centimetre long. Then based on what happens, you can infer the function of the piece in the machine. For example, if the machine falls apart you likely removed a structural component, if the wheel stops turning you might have removed the motor, and so on. Based on the information you compile you draw a model of the machine. This model is then repeatedly tested with more and more specific questions to complete your understanding of what the machine looks like and how it works.

MARIA MACLENNAN

Age: 33
Ethnicity: White, Scottish
Gender and sexuality: Cis Female, Bisexual
Geographical location: Scotland, UK
Current institution: Lecturer in Jewellery and Silversmithing, Edinburgh College of Art (ECA), The University of Edinburgh, Scotland and Service Design Manager, The Police Service of Scotland, Kincardine, Scotland

ABOUT ME

As an only child to a single working-class mother from a Council Estate in the rural Highlands of Scotland; what I lacked in money, I more than made up for in love. My mother, a former Headmistress, worked extremely hard to support my ambition to attend Art College – an education many parents and professionals still dismiss as a 'Mickey Mouse' career. I remain eternally grateful to my mother, and to the network of strong and supportive women throughout my life who have taught me independence, tenacity, creativity, and empathy, and instilled in me the strong work ethic, insatiable thirst for knowledge, and passion for helping others that still inform both my personal and professional working approach.

As a heavily tattooed young women and member of the LQBTQIA+ community also living with several chronic illnesses and poor mental health (high-functioning anxiety,

depression, premenstrual dysphoric disorder, endometriosis and hypothyroidism); I am privileged to occupy a hybrid role as both a Lecturer at a Russell Group University and a Senior Manager within the UK's second-largest police force. I am proud to represent someone of my background and creativity in two traditionally masculine and stoic cultures, which often shun women, poor mental health and the single working class. My aim is to ensure I continue to leave the ladder down to help support other young women to take up more space in these areas in the future.

FUN FACT

- I am tattooed, quite literally, from head-to-toe (on my head, face, neck, hands and other areas I shan't mention).

- Singer Jimmy Osmond once sketched me on live radio (during a guest spot on BBC Radio 4 Saturday Live).

- I was once featured in the popular Ripley's Believe It or Not (next to some KFC-flavoured nail polish).

- My photo was once used in a Reddit thread called 'HumanPorn' ('high quality images of humans not having sex').

- I once called the Queen's Crown Jeweller 'jammy' to his face (during an interview for a scholarship, which incidentally, I didn't get).

MY RESEARCH

Jewellery, like alchemy, is transformed over time. Having originally trained as a jewellery designer and silversmith, I was

inspired to become a researcher to continue to develop new knowledge of jewellery as both a discipline and a medium, pushing the boundaries of design in exploratory and challenging directions and challenging the perceptions of what's possible with an art and design degree.

Rooted in co-design and craft practice, my award-winning research in 'Forensic Jewellery' is the first of its kind in the world, focused on pioneering jewellery's role as an aid in forensic and criminal investigations. Centred upon a highly interdisciplinary portfolio of practice; my current projects include the identification of deceased migrants in the Mediterranean, using the cultural and religious personal property recovered upon their person; the links between jewellery crime and illicit money laundering in Canada, and the effect of jewellery on eyewitness testimony in forensic art and facial reconstructions.

Alongside my research, I have collaborated on a broad portfolio of practice; outside, inside and alongside high-profile organisations across both academia and in the public sector internationally, and currently consult for several law enforcement agencies and non-government organisations. My research outputs are concerned with influencing policy and practice around forensic jewellery and gem crime internationally. This has included contributing to the development of INTERPOL guidelines and educational resources for both law enforcement practitioners and jewellery industry personnel. Passionate about public engagement, I am also a regular contributor to national television and radio and a guest speaker to both design and forensic audiences alike. This has previously included the National Crime Agency, Victoria and Albert Museum, Royal College of Art, Royal Institute of Great Britain and a TEDx talk.

FUN FACT

In 2016, *The Times* newspaper dubbed me 'The World's First Forensic Jeweller', a title that has since been picked up by the *Financial Times*, *New York Times* and *BBC World News*.

In 2021, a short film about my research (THE DEAD ARE JEWELS TO ME) aired on BBC3 for International Woman's Day. It was nominated for 'Best UK Short Film' at London Short Film Festival, and the 'Scotland's Year of Stories Short' Film Award' at Glasgow Short Film Festival (2022).

In 2022, I was shortlisted in the AHRC/BBC New Generation Thinkers Scheme and featured by UK Research and Innovation (UKRI) as part of their documentary series, '101 Jobs that Changed the World'.

ACTIVITY

The Jewellery Autopsy is a research-informed teaching activity run with Y1 students as part of the 'Living Objects: Concept and Narrative' elective at The University of Edinburgh. The activity aims to (gently) introduce jewellery students to theme(s) of forensics, encouraging them to critically question objects and their context(s) beyond initial perceptions and surface-level assumptions.

You too, can run this activity with friends, colleagues or students by following these simple steps:

- Purchase an object (from a charity shop, antiques centre, flea market, eBay, etc.).

- Utilise a variety of tools (scalpel, scissors, glue, ink, sandpaper, etc.) and techniques (colouring, scraping, hammering, sawing, cutting, mark-making, etc.) to begin to 'dissect' the object, wearing it away or breaking it down into fragments. Why not experiment with deconstruction

by burying the object in the earth, submerging it in water, or even reassemble its component parts to create a new form …?

- Present the object/fragments in a mock crime scene scenario, as if it were forensic evidence (think forensic rulers, evidence bags, barcodes, crime scene tape, magnifying glasses, etc.).

- Ask each participant to swap their object/fragments with a partner. Through questions, observation and drawing, participants should attempt to 'reconstruct' each other's object, looking for 'clues' as to its identity. What is/was the object? What might have happened to it? Encourage participants to come up with a narrative to support their theories, investigating detail through drawing while labelling/annotating any interesting features or observations they may notice.

ZARAH PATTISON

Age: 36 … nearly 37.
Ethnicity: I am white but describe myself as white other in the tick boxes. I was born and raised in South Africa, having moved to the UK at 15. I am now privileged to have dual nationality – South African and British.
Gender and sexuality: I am a cisgendered female, heterosexual
Geographical location: I was born in Cape Town, South Africa and currently live in Stirling, Scotland, UK.
Current institution: I work at Newcastle University in England – commuting and living between there and Stirling.

ABOUT ME

I moved to the UK at 15. The UK education system was very different, and my half-shaved head and tattoos did me no favours with the teachers and students. Having been independent from a young age and working in South Africa from 13/14 years old, I struggled to stay in school but managed to scrape through GCSEs (high school exams).

As a teen I had always wanted to be a make-up artist. I started working at Boots in Crawley at 16 as a Beauty Consultant, studying 'Beauty' at college in the evenings. I worked my way up to a position in London for Lancôme at 18 and then to national make-up artist for Clinique at 21.

I remember working in a store one weekend feeling that I wanted something else. I wanted to be outside, exploring! So,

after much searching, I started home studying for an Open University (OU) Diploma in Natural Science, while working full time. I was not a natural academic, scraping through many modules, but I enjoyed it.

Having moved out of home around the age of 19, the idea of leaving my job and going to university wasn't something I had considered, until I went on a lab and field course in person. That one week changed everything. The dynamic learning environment pushed me to apply to universities. One out of four universities accepted me. I gave up my full time, rent paying make-up artist career and started my degree in 2008. I am the first in my family to pursue post-school education.

FUN FACT

When I first started my OU Diploma, I wanted to be a Cheetah rehabilitator – wearing khaki shorts, driving a jeep in SA. I originally signed up for a Zoology degree, but one module on plants, insects and fungi, gave me a new perspective on the natural world. I switched my degree to Ecology, becoming increasingly interested in plants. Now I wear waterproofs, drive a van and search for alien plants along rivers, while frequently falling over in the mud.

I also have a rescue dog called, Ninja. He can almost clear a 6-feet fence when chasing pigeons in the garden.

MY RESEARCH

My area of research is focused on the drivers and impacts of alien species (biological invasions). I am particularly interested in alien plants and how they invade rivers, lakes and wetlands (freshwater habitats). Invasive alien species are spread by humans to areas they would not be able to reach naturally. They are one of the biggest drivers of biodiversity

loss globally therefore, understanding how they arrive, what makes them successful and how they interact with their new environment is important to manage and prevent further invasions.

After my BSc I wanted to do a MSc to continue building my skills for an environment-focused job. I couldn't afford to do a taught MSc, so was restricted to doing a cheaper (at the time) MRes – research masters. By this point in my life, I had to live between two houses and work to carrying on studying. It was worth it. I loved being outside tending to my experiment growing an invasive plant in different soil types to see how it grew and looking for fungi in the plant's roots in the lab. I felt like I was in this hidden world where I shouldn't be. The creative freedom research offers is unlike any other job I had before. My MRes supervisor encouraged me to apply for a PhD and from there I have been trying to keep my foot in this 'hidden' world since.

FUN FACT

Many of the first alien plants were brought to their new 'homes' by 18th century Plant Hunters. These Plant Hunters sought out any potentially valuable plant species to send back

home. This led to botanical gardens and horticulturists competing to bring back the most exotic plant species.

The easiest and fastest growing beautiful plants were prized possessions in large estates. Until 200 years later, when these plants escaped those enclosed gardens, wreaking havoc in their new habitats. The traits that had been selected by the Plant Hunters were also the traits that made these alien plants so successful!

ACTIVITY

Humans have a natural interest in, and a greater empathy for, species with human-like characteristics. Conservation efforts for these types of species are therefore greater. It can be difficult to encourage people's interest in the plants around them. This is often called 'Plant blindness' – 'the inability to see or notice the plants in one's own environment'.

Plants give us the air we breathe! The basic food for all organisms is produced by green plants. More than 28,000 plant species are used medicinally, but we are yet to even discover a large proportion of the world's plant species. Plants are also going extinct faster than we can discover them!

Classes in plant sciences across educational institutions are not generating enough interest from students to remain viable. How can we change this? Encourage people to learn some alternative facts about the plants they see around them.

What is this plant and why is it there?

Head outside to the park, your garden or further afield. Alternatively, pick your house plants or look up some images on the Plantlife charity website: https://www.plantlife.org.uk/uk/discover-wild-plants-nature

Pick three to five plants that look different (different species).

Answer and write down the following:

1. What type of plant is this? (PlantNet app)

2. Where does this plant live (its habitat, grassland, river, etc.)?

3. Is this plant native or an alien?

4. Which animals (bees, deer, etc.) use this plant for food?

5. Fun fact: Is there any folklore associated with this plant (use in magic, medicine, etc.)

BERNADINE JONES

Age: 38
Ethnicity: White South African
Gender and sexuality: Female, Cis, bisexual
Geographical location: Scotland, UK
Current institution: University of Stirling, Scotland, UK

ABOUT ME

I completed my PhD at the University of Cape Town (UCT) in 2018 and was fortunate to secure a permanent position teaching journalism in 2021. I'm a first-generation Early Career Researcher – none of my extended family went to university, and neither of my parents completed traditional high school. Despite this, both parents instilled in me a passion for education and learning from an early age. I worked all the way through my degrees, and during my Masters and PhD tutored undergraduate classes at UCT. Through my supervisor's mentorship, I applied for and was successful in winning a full scholarship for my PhD that enabled me to study full time in the last two years of the degree. I am a Global South researcher, although I am a white South African so have that privilege, and faced numerous problems in attending conferences, getting access to high-ranking journal articles, and getting published because of this geolocation. Moving to the UK in 2017 highlighted this inequality as conference attendance

and journal access is much easier when tied to a Global North university.

FUN FACT

I am a staunch proponent of looking, wearing, talking and being as comes natural to you – I have blue (sometimes pink) hair, visible piercings, am a proud metalhead in all aspects of my life, and often teach in my metal shirts to signal to students that I am a safe person to talk music with. I am out as bi/pansexual (although I am cisgender). What shocks most people when they look at me is that I am also currently working my way up the ladder to professorship – many people cannot unite my appearance with my career, and that's even more reason to dress, talk and act your natural self.

MY RESEARCH

I research visual news, African representation and journalism practice with the underlying method and theory of (social) semiotics. We live in a complicated time, saturated by screens and news media, navigating post-truth politics, and live in a world shaped by the pandemic. There is a crisis in journalism arising from mediatised reporting that is more flashy than informative. Our reliance on visual news is at an all-time high, be that through television broadcasts or video on demand. Yet, if we are to flourish as a society, then we must take more care over these crafted news narratives. Taking visual news seriously is a step in the right direction.

My path to this research focus started on an after-school bus in rural west Wales in 1994. I had recently, but briefly, moved to Wales with my mother. I was the first South African many of my fellow pupils had seen. One question on that bus propelled me to study South African representation into

my adulthood. 'Why aren't you black?'. Surely Welsh children had been exposed to the news of apartheid – there were definitely white people in South Africa, yet this was the foremost question in an 11-year-old's mind. It was a product of popular media and news narratives, and a question that led me to research the representation of South Africa for over two decades.

FUN FACT

When we say, 'a picture is worth a thousand words', and you're trying to write a paper on the semiotics of a TV news broadcast, how many words will you need for something that is four minutes of moving pictures? Definitely more than 10,000 right? WRONG! Semiotic analyses are naturally very wordy, a problem when dealing with moving image media. I developed a methodology to help cut down the words (and the time) it takes to analyse TV news. Using a combination of multimodal, critical discourse and social semiotic analyses, this method can help cut down your word count, your spreadsheets, your NVivo entries and preserve your time and sanity.

ACTIVITY

Visual storytelling is a critical component in news stories today. The way the camera is used (framing, composition and

movement), how the participants on screen are positioned (through an image act of offer or demand), and how colour is used as shorthand (red for danger, red for sexuality and red for war) are all aspects of visual storytelling.

Theorists in this field include:

Kress and Van Leeuwen's reading images.

Gianetti's understanding movies.

Chandler's modes of address in semiotics for beginners.

You can read up on their work and how they analyse images and suggest meanings.

Practical exercise:

Pick some news images – these can be iconic scenes (the Twin Towers disaster in 2001, Nelson Mandela's walk to freedom in 1990 and the fall of the Berlin Wall in 1989) or modern depictions (Clapping for the NHS, wildfires in Australia and Trump's campaign trail). Whatever they are, pick visually 'interesting' images and make a note of the news outlet (e.g. CNN, BBC, or The Guardian).

Consider these techniques: Composition, framing, angles, movement, positioning, and colour.

You may need to research what these techniques mean before you begin.

Questions:

Do you think changing any of the techniques (a different colour, a different angle and a different frame) would change the meaning of the image?

CINDERELLA TEMITOPE OCHU

Age: 34
Ethnicity: I am a Nigerian and from the Yoruba ethnic group
Gender and sexuality: Female. She/Her
Geographical location: South Africa
Current institution: University of Johannesburg, South Africa

ABOUT ME

At the time of writing I am currently a PhD candidate in the Department of History, University of Johannesburg, South Africa. My research centres on histories of reproductive technologies in sub-Saharan Africa in the twentieth century, with a specific focus on Nigeria. I bagged a BA degree in International Studies and Diplomacy and MA in History, University of Benin, Nigeria. My two degrees in unrelated fields make me flexible in research and methodologies. I am passionate about Gender/Women's issues, and the framework of sexual history and developmental studies. Some of my works include:

- *Mortality and Fertility in Sub-Sahara Africa*: Investigating the precautionary measures in Nigeria, 1960s–c. 1990s.

- *'Depo' and Development in Sub-Sahara Africa*: Investigating women and contraceptive technologies in Nigeria 1960s–1990s.

- *Women, Development and Inequality in Edo State, Nigeria*: A sociological perspective.

I have also attended and presented papers in both local and international conferences such as the 19th Annual Africa Conference held at the University of Texas, Austin, USA (in-person), and completed some virtual trainings and obtained certificates from institutions like the University of Glasgow and London School of Hygiene and Tropical Medicine. Prior to my Masters, I worked as a journalist with Newswatch Communications Ltd, the first Nigerian news magazine, where I developed an interest in research. My diversity is further reflected in my ability to publish my research in the media.

FUN FACT

Back in high school, I enjoyed writing poems but later gave up on the hobby after comparing my poem to that of a friend who was a poet and I noticed the difference. She was very skilful in the art and mine was no match. As an undergraduate, I loved to read Mills & Boon novels, not anymore. I guess I do not have time for that again, or perhaps, a change in priorities. What I enjoy doing in my spare time now is to watch movies, comedy to be precise. I also love music and dance a great deal!

MY RESEARCH

My research area focuses on birth control/contraception and family planning in Sub-Saharan Africa. In researching these areas, themes such as marriage, fertility/pregnancy and reproduction often come up. My motivation for the study emerged from the reality that my country, Nigeria, is fast becoming the most populous country in Africa, with heightened poverty and mortality rates. Yet, family planning programmes and services are in place and contraceptives are in fact distributed

for free at medical centres. I was curious to know the reason behind the phenomenon and thus, embarked on an academic enquiry. I travelled to Nigeria this year (2021) and conducted an in-depth interview with 67 women. The participants were very engaging and opened up on many areas of their lives. They answered questions about their reproductive decisions, contraceptive choices and childbearing. At some points, the interviews became emotional as they recounted their traumatic experiences like divorce/separation resulting from lack of a male child. I gathered from the interviews that socio-cultural practices, such as the premium placed on children/large family size, preference for a gender/sex role, patriarchy and religious injunctions against artificial contraception, are factors fuelling population growth in the country.

FUN FACT

My fieldwork was a unique experience for me. Although there were some teary moments, the fun part of it came when the participants talked about sexual intercourse with their partners; the women laughed and made jokes about it. For instance, I find the moniker 'fila daddy' (daddy's cap) or 'ade daddy' (daddy's crown) given to condoms hilarious. Another amusing incident occurred when several women revealed where they used to hide their contraceptives to prevent their spouse from seeing them. Some mentioned places like under the bed, inside the pot and so on.

ACTIVITY

According to studies, total fertility rates in Sub-Saharan Africa were high in the 1960s and 1970s. The adoption of family system in which large numbers of children were culturally valued for economic gains and prestige, was a common

practice in the region. During this time, children benefitted their parents and households in both economic and non-economic ways. Male children assist in farm work while daughters bring wealth through bride price. Sons were appreciated as they ensured the continuity of the family name and perpetuated the lineage while daughters rendered support at old age. Although, children were generally cherished for security and marital stability, in a traditional setting and patriarchal society like Africa, sons were regarded as more productive (agriculture) and equally demonstrated the masculinity of men. In recent times, with the increase in female education and employment, and advancement in technology, the fertility rate is predicted to decline drastically. Contrarily, in some parts of the continent, especially in Nigeria, there is still a predilection for large families. The main question that arises therefore is:

What were the motivations for the practice of large family size in Sub-Saharan Africa?

To answer the above, can you explore the following questions:

- What were the values placed on children?

- How do parental expectations, sex roles and gender preferences affect fertility?

- What were the systems put in place to sustain these practices?

- To what extent has development in the twenty-first century influenced these practices?

MELISSA ANNE BEATTIE

Age: 42
Ethnicity: White/Jewish
Gender and sexuality: Ciswoman, queer (aromantic asexual)
Geographical location: Yerevan, Armenia
Current institution: Assistant Professor of English and Comms, American University of Armenia

ABOUT ME

I'm an openly queer, assertive Jewish woman who switched disciplines at 32 during a disastrous PhD-turned-MPhil. I ultimately ended up getting my PhD at 38, almost 20 years to the day after I started my undergraduate degree. I've been openly queer (aro/ace) since I understood what that meant (which took until my 30s), even in very conservative countries and environments. It's important for my queer students (out and not) to have role models and, while calling my career 'successful' is a very generous assessment, I'm at least able to show my students and my colleagues someone who managed to get to the front of a classroom while also being 'different'.

FUN FACT

I have nine (soon to be 10) tattoos. They're all from places I've lived and/or travelled.

MY RESEARCH

I research discursive constructions of national and subnational identities, media representation and audience reception/interpretation. I became a researcher mostly out of spite, in the sense that I was told by a bad supervisor that I couldn't write a PhD that was good enough to pass and, even if I could do that, it wouldn't be good enough to get me a job. I disagreed and decided that I wanted to help that sort of thing not happen again to anyone. I switched to Media Studies and learnt about how intersectional identities and oppressions work and both why and how representation matters. I then decided that continuing to learn about that, teach about that and speak about that, to any audience who would listen, was the best way I could contribute to global society.

FUN FACT

I also engage in media practice, primarily theatre. I have had two performances produced in the UK, one in Korea and directed one in Korea. These experiences have deepened my understanding of media theory, industry and practice and my understanding of audiences has helped me improve my produced works.

ACTIVITY

You can do this activity in a class or as an individual. The goal is to become more media literate about how much representation matters.

- Type the names of jobs that you would like to have into Google Images and see what kinds of images come up. You can make a poster of these if you like.

- Consider and/or label the gender, race and any other identities shown in the images.

- Importantly, what identities don't you see?

- If you are in a group discuss why you think that might be.

SARAH MOHAMMAD-QURESHI

Age: 42
Ethnicity: British Pakistani
Gender and sexuality: Heterosexual woman
Geographical location: Greater Manchester, UK
Current institution: The University of Law, UK

ABOUT ME

'Diverse' is an interesting word, diverse from whom? I share many characteristics with the majority in the sector but then also identify with some less abundant characteristics. It's that combination which gives us all our unique identities and, effectively, makes us all diverse from one another. I'm a second generation British Pakistani who grew up in one of the most deprived towns in the UK. Some of my earliest memories are linked to racist abuse around the estate and the generous use of the P-word in primary school, so I was well-aware of being ethnically 'different' from a very young age. I didn't necessarily take those experiences as indicative of society telling me I couldn't do or be anything, in fact there was little evidence that I was less capable than anyone, it was just words and actions which were just part of the environment. Further into my education and career, I've become accustomed to being the ethnic minority. Entering the research pathway was interesting – the non-white researchers were almost entirely overseas students and we had very different life

experiences, yet the general feeling was that we were grouped as one 'BAME' group with a shared identity. I again found myself quite isolated – coming from a low socioeconomic background definitely limited my connection with my peers too, regardless of ethnicity – I had regular 'banter' about my accent and inferred links to intellect, which I laughed off for far too long in an attempt to fit in.

FUN FACT

In 2016, at the age of 37 I decided to train in martial arts. I took up karate, having never tried it before and worked my way through the grading system. I continued (non-contact) training throughout my pregnancy and in 2018 I had my baby and graded for my next belt three months later! I achieved my Brown belt in 2019 just before the pandemic and frustratingly would have been on track to grade for my Black belt in 2021 if the dojo hadn't been closed for much of the pandemic.

MY RESEARCH

My research career started in Science. After initially undertaking a PhD to develop my applied skills, I continued as a biochemical researcher for almost 15 years, working on the childhood brain disease Leukoencephalopathy with Vanishing White Matter. I absolutely loved the freedom of following my curiosities and deciphering evidence, however the option to continue with that area of research was becoming difficult. The major funding bodies gave greater focus to those research areas which had wider impact than research into a rare disease would be expected to deliver, and structural barriers interfered with my personal progression in the traditional academic research route; I left the bench in 2015.

Now I contribute to research in different ways, I've worked in equality, diversity and inclusion in higher education since 2016, researching issues impacting on specific groups of people, reviewing emerging research and best practice, undertaking quantitative and qualitative data analysis, and evaluating impact. I also work for two equality charities and am involved in contributing to active/future research in their areas of focus.

It took a while to accept not being a researcher when I left the academic pipeline, however lately I have realised that there are more ways to contribute and undertake research outside of those traditional roles and so much of what I do uses the same investigative and reasoning skills.

FUN FACT

My work combines many subject areas, which I never expected to work in. I always thought I struggled with Maths, yet so much of my work involves data analysis and manipulation – I realise now I needed to experience the application of Maths in real life to gain and appreciate and enjoyment for it. I certainly couldn't do my work without it! I also use my English language skills for communicating information and for ensuring there is no ambiguity when collecting evidence. The work brings in elements of Social Sciences, Psychology, Education, etc., too, it is so varied and never boring.

ACTIVITY

We often feel that we live along a path that we have had major influence in creating:

Everything, from our education choices/careers/where we live/who we socialise with, being a conscious decision. However, what we don't often realise is who or what influences those decisions.

This could be a workshop with a class or group (including family members or people you live with). I want you to explore your route to the current day, to evidence how easy it is to reverse decisions or make changes when it comes to your career. This might be about what you are studying right now or what job you have or what career you want in the future. It's a great exercise to take the apparent emotion away from career decisions but also to explore 'privilege' – what/who did you have as resources to help you achieve these milestones.

Activity: I am going to guide you to unravel key milestones in your life and reflect on how you arrived at that point:

- List or draw your significant milestones in a timeline or thoughtshower.

- On this image add all the resources that helped you to get there. This might include things like people, cost, transport, advice, etc.

- Who or what helped you get there and decide where to go next?

MANDY HUGHES

Age: 51
Ethnicity: Australian
Gender and sexuality: Female, heterosexual
Geographical location: Coffs Harbour, Northern New South Wales, regional (non-metropolitan) Australia
Current institution: Southern Cross University, Australia

ABOUT ME

I was the first in my family to study at university, coming from a working-class background. I came to academia from a non-traditional path, growing up in country town and leaving school at age 16 to commence a hairdressing apprenticeship. I returned to school the following year and later went on to university study. After university, I worked in various sectors, including women's refuges/women's housing (for Culturally and Linguistically Diverse clients), followed by a nearly 10-year career in television (public broadcasting) working mostly on political news in Australia's Parliament House. After doing some sessional tutoring at university, I decided to pursue education and commenced study for a secondary teaching qualification. I taught media studies and social sciences in schools for four years and then returned to the community sector to work in international and community development. This included a project based in Southeast Asia as an Advisor to Lao National Television. In 2008, after

relocating to be closer to family, I transitioned into university teaching across a range of subjects including social sciences, social welfare and media studies. My life experience informs my work as a researcher and educator. This includes being the mother of two children, one of whom has a disability. My work is embedded in social justice principles where I seek to understand and advocate for diverse community members to promote social inclusion.

FUN FACT

I worked in television for nearly 10 years before crossing over to education. Being based in Australia's Parliament House, I got to see behind the scenes of politics in action. During this time, I travelled domestically and overseas to record, sound and edit stories about political events like the South Pacific Forum in the Cook Islands. During this trip, political delegates travelled to a retreat on a small out-lying island. Media crews did not have transport organised for the return trip and we hitched a ride with the New Zealand Airforce on their Hercules aircraft – the plane had no seats and we were strapped into harnesses. An exciting return trip.

MY RESEARCH

My research focuses on marginalised communities, including refugees and regional youth in locationally disadvantaged regions. I use creative and visual research methods to link communities and go beyond traditional notions of research. As part of my PhD, I made a film called *The last refuge: food stories from Myanmar to Coffs Harbour*. The film, about how cultural foods can bring people together and reconnect them to traditions, was screened in film

festivals in Europe, North America, Australia and Central America. A more recent project saw a five-year collaboration with a community organisation to document and evaluate a programme for women from refugee and migrant backgrounds. I made multiple films about the programme and collaborated with staff and participants to produce a 150-page full-colour book telling the women's stories. I also initiated the idea to hold public exhibitions at multiple locations to invite visitors to engage with diverse communities, members and learn about their life experiences. This project has received numerous awards for research impact, and findings have been shared widely.

I have always loved research. In my roles in television, I researched current social issues to produce high quality, ethical television programmes. I also utilised research skills in community and international development to design, implement, monitor and evaluate programmes. My work in education has always required well-developed research skills to create relevant and engaging curricula for students. My passion for research came full circle when I completed my PhD in 2017 and I continue producing socially engaged, collaborative research with diverse communities. I believe research should be accessible and relevant to real-world problems and lived experiences.

FUN FACT

The most fulfilling part of making films collaboratively with research participants is being with them at a public screening and seeing how proud they are to tell their own stories about their culture.

ACTIVITY

How could you tell your story through film? We all have access to a phone these days and can put together a short film in no time. Think about a social issue that concerns you in your local community. Spend some time scouting for locations. Record your commentary and/or interview family and friends about your issue. Edit your film with free video editing software (iMovie or MovieMaker or other). If you haven't done this before, there are heaps of video editing tutorials online. Share your research findings in your finished video via social media or your preferred method.

JASMINE HAZEL SHADRACK

Age: 44
Ethnicity: Mixed white other
Gender and sexuality: Cis, bi
Geographical location: Northamptonshire, UK
Current institution: Visiting Lecturer at Falmouth University, UK, BIMM Berlin, Germany, and the University of Central Missouri, USA

ABOUT ME

I'm a heavily tattooed, late-diagnosed neurodivergent academic who specialises in trauma studies, performance studies, disability studies, extreme metal, musicology, autoethnography and psychoanalysis.

I was a Senior Lecturer in popular music for 13 years until I left last August. Now I do Visiting Lecturer work at the above institutions alongside working for The Work Inclusion Project. My monograph entitled *Black Metal, Trauma, Subjectivity and Sound: Screaming the Abyss* was published in January (2021) through Emerald Publishing and I am currently co-editing the next Music and Death book with Dr Marie Josephine Bennet (University of Winchester) and Dr Gary Levy (Deakin University, Australia) also through Emerald, *Death and the Senses* with Dr Christina Welch (University of Winchester) through Equinox and the very first ever edited

collection on metal music culture and disability entitled *Crips, Crowds and Cacophony: Dis/Ability in Metal Music* through Intellect Books with Dr Keith Kahn-Harris. I am a Member of the National Coalition for Independent Scholars and the Secretary of its UK subsidiary FIRE UK. I also sit on the Board for the International Society for Metal Music Studies and the new Advances in Metal Music and Culture series through Intellect.

I am late-diagnosed autistic and ADHD, with accompanying C-post-traumatic stress disorder (PTSD) and fibromyalgia. To students, I don't look like I'm part of the system which has really helped them to see that you can have control over your own subjectivity. Learning about my neurodiversity when I was 43 changed everything. I always knew I was different, but I thought that there was something inherently wrong with me, which I now know is a common feeling in the neurodivergent community. It has split my life into a before and an after. Now, I am coming to understand what my appearance, presence, research and teaching style really means in an environment that makes no reasonable adjustments.

FUN FACT

- I am a guitarist and front woman in the black metal band Denigrata – and am now part of a blackened folk duo with Francesca Stevens called Dōloŭr that we began during lockdown.

- I live on a narrowboat that my husband and I bought four years ago as a renovation project! Still a way to go but she's beautiful!

- We have a rescue Dalmatian called Mr Pants!

- I'm composing a Requiem Mass for full choir and orchestra. I'm roughly halfway through.

MY RESEARCH

I was lecturing full time when I was first prompted to start researching as part of my continuing professional development (CPD) and I have been doing so since 2014.

I am an autoethnographer (research my own life experiences), for the most part. It started when I survived domestic abuse and found that therapy was not working for me, so I started Denigrata. This then became the focus of my PhD (2017) and then my monograph (book) in 2021. I am immensely proud of this. I used my experiences of domestic abuse and applied them to the band by using Interpretive Performance Autoethnography. It has since been noted by Prof. Lori Burns (*Disruptive Divas*, Routledge, 2002) and Laina Dawes (*What Are You Doing Here? A Black Woman's Life and Liberation in Heavy Metal*, Bazillion Points Press, 2012) that I have created a new paradigm (model to investigate or explain).

I am currently branching out into Death Studies and Disability Studies.

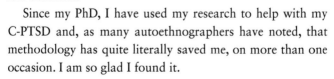

I have been told that my research is 'academic prose', which comes from my love of Julia Kristeva and Walter Benjamin. It's a heavy, poetic writing style that is as rigorous as it is beautiful.

Since my PhD, I have used my research to help with my C-PTSD and, as many autoethnographers have noted, that methodology has quite literally saved me, on more than one occasion. I am so glad I found it.

FUN FACT

As part of my PhD research, Denigrata wrote, recorded and produced an album (available here Missa Defunctorum: Requiem Mass in A Minor|Denigrata (bandcamp.com)) and a video (included above!).

My research tends towards the miserable end of things, so I at least try to make the language pretty!

ACTIVITY

You can explore how song writers write about their own lives as a form of autoethnography. Think of musicians you like to listen to and if they write about their own life experience. Think about how those lyrics might be saying something about their lived experience.

Demonstrate how you have come to understand your own subjectivity (the way you are in the world). You can do this by writing a piece of creative writing, poem or song lyric about experiences in your own life.

JENNIFER LEIGH

Age: 45 (though I have told my kids I am 100 for the last 23 years)

Ethnicity: I am Jewish. I always write this as my ethnicity as being Jewish is more than being part of a minority religion, it is being part of a culture and a people. I grew up in an area where there were not very many other Jews. I was the only one in my school of more than 800 girls. I am not particularly religious, and yet for most of my life I have hidden my ethnicity and 'passed' for fear of antisemitism.

Gender and sexuality: I am pretty much heterosexual.

Geographical location: South East UK

Current institution: University of Kent, UK

ABOUT ME

My route into academia was unconventional. I started university age 17 studying Chemistry. I became pregnant in my second year, and while friends had a year out in industry or abroad, I had a baby. I finished my degree, applied for teacher training, but took up a funded PhD in computational chemistry.

My supervisor left for industry promising to continue externally and passed me over to a friend in a different area. The external supervision did not pan out, and I had to find another project within my new supervisor's expertise after a year.

My daughter was hospitalised for bronchiolitis then pneumonia, and these triggered extreme eczema. I went part-time against the wishes of the head of department. When I became pregnant with my second child the university offered a three-month unpaid extension, and eventually I was technically expelled.

During this time, I trained as a yoga teacher, and after leaving the university began somatic movement therapist training and worked privately, for SureStart centres, and Primary Care Trusts.

I embarked on a part-time PhD looking at how children experienced their sense of embodiment. Embodiment means how you express yourself and ideas through your body/self – your state of being. In the following four years I moved across the country, got divorced, completed a PGCE in secondary science, the PhD, found work as a postdoctoral researcher in psychology, and completed a PGCHE.

Eventually I secured a lectureship in higher education. The birth of my third child was traumatic and resulted in chronic ill health and disability. Through COVID-19 I learned that I am autistic and have ADHD.

FUN FACT

- I have a hand-poked tattoo of cherry blossom that runs from my lower left arm to the top of my right hip that has been featured in a book.

- I worked as a knit designer, and have published patterns in several international magazines.

- I used to be able to do the splits (and would love to be able to again but have been stuck at about an inch above the floor for a few years).

- I have grade 8 flute and ice-skating.

- I have two ducks, two chickens, a fat cat and a fluffy dog.

MY RESEARCH

My work is threaded together by a vision to make academia a better, kinder place. I use Embodied *inquiry* which foregrounds lived experiences, and research on creative research methods.

I am a Vice Chair of the International Women in Supramolecular Chemistry (WISC) network which launched late 2019, and brings a social science and equality, diversity and inclusion (EDI) perspective to work with scientists to address marginalisation. I lead a programme of public engagement and research that embeds creativity and reflexive practice into teams to enhance communication. My collaborative autoethnography group for chemists has had a positive impact on the members' research outputs and grant successes. A book from WISC will be published by Policy Press in 2022.

As a disabled woman, I want to embed accessibility into science and higher education. There is a common perception that only students are disabled/chronically ill/neurodivergent, and numbers of staff declaring disability/chronic illness/neurodivergence is less than 4%, compared to estimates of up to 30% within the general population. WISC are leading a project on accessible labs for the future, and I co-lead the National Association for Disabled Networks' STEMM Action Group which has produced a problem statement and has already been invited to talk to funders and institutions in the UK. My work on ableism in academia includes an open access book *Ableism in Academia* (UCL Press).

Although the bodies of work on ableism and WISC are relatively recent, there have already been tangible benefits for staff and students at Kent, WISC members, and the wider scientific community.

FUN FACT

It is well recognised that chemistry has a gender imbalance. It is less well known that this is not due to women and girls not being interested. Women have always been interested in science, but they have not always had the opportunities for work and recognition.

In 2020 about half of chemistry undergraduates in the UK were women. The issue is with retention and progression. The biggest attrition happens post-PhD, and in the UK less than 9% of full professors of chemistry are women.

Calling on the community, reflecting and increasing a sense of kinship is helping to effect change.

ACTIVITY

I use creative and embodied approaches to elicit stories that are deeper, more emotional, and more honest than those on the surface. Think about the way that you introduce yourself if you are in a group – it is likely to be functional, who you are, what you do and where you are from. Instead, imagine bringing an object or an image that represents who you are, telling the story behind that, and hearing other people's stories, seeing their objects, asking questions and finding resonances.

This is an activity that needs to be boundaried. If the question is too big or too wide it can take you to places that you may not be comfortable sharing.

Within a group I suggest the question is not 'who are you?' but 'who are you as...?'. For example, I have used 'who are

you as ... a chemist?', '... a dancer?', '... a teacher?' and '... a researcher?'. It is important to be aware of the time that the activity can take, making sure that any group is not too big so that everyone gets a chance to share and to be heard.

The activity could be extended by creating an installation or image that incorporates all the things that people shared, either post-haste or participatively, and can be used to disseminate people's lived experiences visually.

Another option is to provide Lego, or high-quality art materials, and ask people to build or draw a response before sharing what it represents to them.

CHIOMA VIVIAN NGONADI

Age: 39
Ethnicity: Nigerian/African
Gender and sexuality: Female
Geographical location: United Kingdom
Current institution: University of Cambridge, UK

ABOUT ME

I was born and raised in south-eastern Nigeria and bagged a
First Class Honours degree in Archaeology from University
of Nigeria, Nsukka. In 2010, I completed an MA in Archaeology from the University of Dar-es-Salaam, Tanzania funded
by SIDA/SAREC through the African Archaeology Network.
After my master's degree and on my return to Nigeria, I
joined the academic staff of the Department of Archaeology, University of Nigeria, Nsukka. My MA research was
on a comparative study of the pottery from sites in coastal
Tanzania. Subsequently, I got admitted into the University
of Cambridge for a PhD in Archaeology under the prestigious Gates Cambridge Scholarship. My PhD application to
Cambridge was very highly rated and I received a full award
from the Gates Cambridge Trust. This achievement in this
highly competitive and prestigious competition is more
remarkable in that I am one of only three scholars from
Africa to have received the Gates Cambridge Scholarship in
2015. My PhD research focused on ancient food production

and subsistence practices among the early iron age, using community in Lejja, south-eastern Nigeria. One of the key aims of my research is to examine the deep time complexity to settlement and plant food production from different occupation horizons through archaeological excavations and flotation. Archaeological flotation is a laboratory technique used to recover tiny artefacts and plant remains from soil samples. I am one of the founding members of the European Society of Black and Allied Archaeologists (ESBAA) and an Associate Editor of the Society for Archaeological Science Bulletin (Archaeobotany section).

FUN FACT

I like organising public engagement outreach events by creating novel, fun and engaging activities for members of the public in Nigeria and the UK.

MY RESEARCH

I am an African Archaeologist and a Lecturer at the Department of Archaeology, University of Nigeria, Nsukka, Nigeria.

I work on seeds, potsherds and charcoal, and in archaeology, these three proxies can help to reconstruct the plant food exploited, vegetation, climate and human–landscape relationship in the deeper past. Growing up as a girl in Nigeria, I was always fascinated by science, innovations and technology. I have also been inspired by women, especially women from patriarchal societies who have worked so hard to overcome their challenging backgrounds and have excelled as astronomers, ecologists, physicists, among others. As a result, I was motivated and encouraged to walk in the footsteps of these

women and this inspired me to become a researcher/archaeologist. I am concerned about the dwindling state of Archaeology in Nigeria as more attention is given to oil and gas exploration and tourism development, Archaeology needs to be preserved and protected not least because it has so much to contribute to sustainable development and education in Africa.

FUN FACT

In south-eastern Nigeria, scientific studies on ancient food production and plant exploitation are very few and most based on hypothetical assumption, oral history and ethnographic data. My research is the first thorough archaeological investigation on food production and subsistence practices among the early iron using communities in south-eastern Nigeria. Using archaeobotany methods, my study pioneered the understanding of subsistence practices and food economy in south-eastern Nigeria by bringing to light how West African iron smelters sustained life and navigated with the quest for food in antiquity.

I find it fascinating that these archaeological materials, which include intricately decorated potsherds, carbonised plants remains, charcoal and iron working remains recovered from archaeological survey, excavations and flotation, can reveal so much about what happened thousands of years ago and can help us link the past to the future.

ACTIVITY

Interested in the past? Take us back to the past from prehistory to the present showing how people's lives have changed through the available material culture.

In answering this question you have to firstly define what archaeology is and how archaeologists find out about what happened in the past which is primarily through the excavation of sites and the analysis of artefacts and other physical remains.

Archaeologists dig up what people in the past have left behind – they use this evidence to find out about their lives; everything they did.

For this task, I want you to look at the things that happened a long time ago.

That could be thousands of years ago (prehistory) when people made use of stone tools, 500 years ago (Tudors) and work through the timeline briefly, giving a sense of change that links the past to the future. Metal was discovered. Towns and cities grew gradually, then quickly with new science and technology. Until we end up in 2021.

JESSICA (JESS) MANNION

Age: 41
Ethnicity: I have white skin with lots of tattoos!
Gender and sexuality: I am a heterosexual woman (she/her).
Geographical location: I live in Sligo, a small town in the North-West of Ireland. I am originally from Leeds, England, UK.
Current institution: I am a full-time Lecturer in Social Sciences, in the Institute of Technology Sligo, Northern Ireland, UK. I also work in Trinity College Dublin, as an Adjunct Teaching Fellow in Disability Studies, and in the same university where I'm doing my PhD as part-time.

ABOUT ME

I dropped out of school when I was 15. I have ADHD, which was undiagnosed at the time. I am also from a working-class background. I do not fit the stereotype of an academic. I am also alternative, with lots of tattoos, and although my hair is black at the minute, I often have two tone hair. I wear alternative clothes, a mix of goth, rock, grunge, rockabilly – depending on my mood. It does not matter what you look like, if you have a disability or where you are from, you can still work in academia. It does not change your ability to do the job better. Unfortunately, some people do judge those that are different, especially in a middle-class institution. Many people hold misconceptions about people with ADHD and their abilities.

The traditional school system did not work for me. I am so glad that I found my way back to education as a mature student. I now have eight higher education qualifications, am working towards my PhD and lecture in two universities. I have also published academically and work as a peer reviewer for two international journals. I now love education and it has changed my life. It has been a challenge, but I am extra proud of myself as a result. At first, I had little confidence in myself and felt that I did not fit into academia. Now I have decided to march to the beat of my own drum!

FUN FACT

My hobbies include reading books and creative writing. I read memoirs, thrillers and romance mainly. My favourite authors are Colleen Hoover, Kristin Hannah, Caroline Kepnes and Alex Michaelides. Currently, I am writing my own memoir about my challenging life background and experiences, and how I have managed to turn my life around. I participate in creative writing classes and am in a writing group. After beginning training to be an ADHD coach, I decided to publish a chapter on how I have used my strengths of ADHD to help me to write, in the hope that it will help others.

MY RESEARCH

I am working with a team of co-researchers who all have intellectual disabilities. We are doing research on relationships and sexuality in their lives. The research team share control of the decisions in the study, such as what topics we explore and how we collect the data. The research team also analyse the data and present the findings. I wanted to do research in this way because I believe that research should be more accessible

to participants. I want to break down power barriers, because the participants are the experts in their own lives. This is also a type of research called 'action research'. Action research is a cycle of action or inquiry that typically follows a process that is repeated over time which usually looks like this – *Identify a problem to be studied. Collect data on the problem. Organise, analyse and interpret the data.*

We are hoping that we can bring about change on the issues our research participants identify.

I have always wanted to make a change for disabled people because I believe they do not have the same equal status in life as non-disabled people. I used to work in the disability sector but felt I could not make enough change there. Research is powerful as it can facilitate people's voices being heard on a wider level. As a result, we can work together to change people's attitudes and identify barriers for people with intellectual disabilities.

When I went back to college as a mature student I stayed after my degree to do research. I found some supportive academic role models on the way who believed in me. I also believed in myself. It has been a challenge financially, having to juggle working while studying, but I love research, so it has been worth it.

FUN FACT

I never imagined the topic of 'the influence of Grand Theft Auto on people with intellectual disabilities perceptions of sex workers' would come up in the research. I would never have researched this if I had not worked with the team as co-researchers and asked them what they wanted to look at. This is so interesting and shows why this participatory method works. People have different opinions about this topic. There are other research studies that have looked at this topic but

none of them are looking at the perceptions of people with intellectual disabilities.

ACTIVITY

When we participate in our research team meetings, we explore the topics in creative ways. The group pick a topic to research. Some of the topics we have researched include finding a boyfriend/girlfriend, LGBTQI+, relationships and sexuality education, dating apps, online safety, marriage, having children, video gaming and sex work. We then choose a creative method to explore this by making up a rap about the topic.

Recently week the group chose marriage. I made a TV out of a cardboard box. I played the opening music of the news. We split up into two groups and each group was asked if they were on the news and could report anything they would like to tell the public in relation to marriage for people with intellectual disabilities, what would it be? Each group prepared a news report to present back to the wider group. After this presentation the group had a good discussion on the topic. Research can be creative, fun and engaging, and by using these methods it really helps to facilitate discussion.

Try these creative methods to explore a topic and see where it takes you. In my opinion, the most fun method is a rap battle. I recommend wearing a baseball cap sideways and a pair of shades for full effect!

LIZA BETTS

Age: 50
Ethnicity: White/British
Gender and sexuality: Female/heterosexual
Geographical location: London, UK
Current institution: University of the Arts, London, UK

ABOUT ME

I grew up and still live in one of the most impoverished London boroughs – Barking and Dagenham (I've moved about but returned here). I attended the local comprehensive school in the early 1980s while feeling the implications and repercussions of Thatcher's Britain emerging. I am the first person in my family to attend university and I only did that as a mature student, I was not able to go at 18. I worked at the Ministry of Defence for a while and then returned to study at Central St Martins School of Art (I had failed my art A Level, so this was quite a big deal for me). I then went on to achieve a Higher National Diploma (HND) in theatre costume. Subsequently I went on to have a 15-year long creative industry career in film and TV costume. When I became a mother, I was unable to continue doing the job I loved. I went back to university and completed a master's degree then went on to begin a PhD (now in my final year – breaks due to illness/pregnancy).

I represent diversity in terms of my social class, my gender, my educational journey, my career trajectory, my life choices and most importantly my lived experience.

I am a working-class women/mother/creative/researcher/lecturer/carer/feminist.

FUN FACT

I've had the good/mis-fortune to work with several 'famous' faces as a costumier. Once I was sent to the home of a very famous actress to pack her suitcase containing costumes hired for a Broadway show. It was not part of my usual role to see actors in their domestic environment and certainly not to witness the usual chaos/stress preparing for a trip abroad – very illuminating. Afterwards, the company driver and I ate a bacon sandwich in a greasy spoon café on Shepherds Bush green and I remember thinking what physically close but experientially distinct lives are experienced simultaneously.

MY RESEARCH

My research has developed into a number of distinct yet connected strands.

My PhD research looks at the language of clothing employed in television drama to produce representations of the working class. I integrate both theory and ethnographic research around creative practice to position contemporary costumed screen representations of 'the ordinary' firmly within the fields of cultural and class politics. I examine how representations of the working class produced ostensibly for the working class, are actually tools of oppression that seek to marginalise and pathologize class experience while simultaneously managing the notion of moral worth. I actively reflect on my own class and creative experiences throughout the research process.

The second strand of my research draws upon experiences of engaging with working-class university students over

the past 10 years and
examines how the concep-
tual space of learning is
framed by class experience
and early childhood development and often managed
via the language of the cur-
riculum to exclude certain
forms of knowledge and
experience that have not
been legitimised by the
establishment.

Finally, I research my role as a mother and the relationships I have had/have with women, mothers/grandmothers in
my family to explore the histories of working-class women's
experiences of motherhood through dress/fashion/style and
how these experiences intersect with narratives of resistance
to gender and class positioning.

I also research working-class masculinity via the culture of
football and footballers.

FUN FACT

I think of my continuing PhD (final year, fingers crossed) as
an epic journey, like Marco Polo on the Silk Road. It has
seen and had to weather many storms experienced by me or
those I love and care for including miscarriage, pregnancy
and birth, redundancy, first academic role, cancer, depression,
anxiety, changing supervisors, an eating disorder, broken
limbs, appendicitis, separation, reconciliation, forced removal
of inspirational Dos' and a global pandemic. Despite everything including the struggle to complete, the subject and my
understanding, knowledge and passion of/for it has remained
my soft place to fall and where I feel safe.

ACTIVITY

The task would explore positionality, subjectivity and the language of established representations.

I would provide participants with a range of 'scripted' scenes, some familiar and some not, and ask the participants to 'costume' the characters that appear on the page – in descriptive format only.

We would then reflectively unpack the thought processes undertaken or the reference points employed and consider the outcomes in relation to subject position, existing representations or the use of familiar tropes or markers.

The purpose would be to make visible and interrogate the language of clothing employed, and the subjectivity inevitably embedded within representations.

We might also go on to consider the 'lived experience' implications of familiar and possibly damaging screen representations.

We would produce visual material, research and mood boards that would articulate the research and reflection process and offer suggestions for the final costumed 'look'.

RHYS ARCHER

Ethnicity: White British
Gender and sexuality: Woman, bisexual
Geographical location: Sheffield, UK
Current institution: The University of Manchester, UK

ABOUT ME

I am autistic. I was diagnosed later in life (age 30) and can see the ways in which a misunderstanding of autism, as well as entrenched ableist attitudes (including my own internalised ableism) has created barriers in both my professional and personal life. Particularly since my diagnosis, I have become an advocate for understanding, and change, towards people with disability, and would love to use this as a platform to be able to further help people understand how people like me experience the world, and simple accommodations that can help prevent the barriers I have experienced.

Additionally, as a woman in STEM (Science, Technology, Engineering, and Mathematics), I have experienced sexism and sexual harassment that have created barriers to my career. This has compounded my experience as an autistic woman and has made navigating the academic world challenging at times. When I was 25, I launched a campaign called Women of Science, to help: (1) provide relatable and diverse STEM women role models to younger people and children; (2) support current people who identify as women, who work in STEM fields; and (3) challenge the perception of what a

scientist or engineer is to the public. The campaign is run voluntarily, based wholly on successful funding bids. Through this I have developed not just a greater understanding of the issues that affect me as a disabled woman in STEM, but also wider intersectional issues. I am so happy to be part of this project to tell my story as a disabled woman in STEM research.

FUN FACT

I can't eat sugar! I have a very rare metabolic disorder called hereditary fructose intolerance (HFI), which means that I wasn't born with the enzymes to break down fructose, sucrose and sorbitol. This means that I can't eat foods such as eat fruit, most vegetables or chocolate! Luckily (ironic) for me, my mum, who has a rare genetic mutation, met my dad, who has a different but equally rare genetic mutation, and together had a 25% chance of a having a child with HFI – of which both my brother and I do! Due to the rarity, we were only diagnosed around six years ago. What is interesting, is that although my sister-in-law does not have the genetic mutation, my nephew is now showing signs that he also has HFI – which goes against all the research there is on it! It makes for many repetitive explanations when eating out with friends, and very laborious conversations with restaurants!

MY RESEARCH

I currently research scaffolds using biocompatible materials for use in tissue engineering. My research journey has been a weird one (although perhaps most would say that!). My interests began with Physics, which morphed into Textile Science and Engineering, I then studied my PhD in composite materials, before switching to Tissue Engineering.

I have always liked to think, and most would say I do too much of it, I think that's why I became a researcher. I also need the degree of freedom and flexibility that a research career (particularly in academia) offers – being autistic, I struggle to keep 'usual' working hours, and can have large amounts of

time where I am unable to work due to over stimulation or sensory overload. Being a researcher means that I can work towards my aims in a way that suits my disability and create an environment that supports and maximises my knowledge and ability, and still be valued for my input. Additionally, one of my autistic behaviours is to become very excited about new and different projects, being a researcher allows me to pick up these projects (such as Women of Science) as and when they come to me and run 100 mph towards them. Unfortunately, I have found that it isn't common to find that type of flex-ibility in other careers, though perhaps that is changing post-pandemic (whenever that is). I would say though, mainly, I chose to be a researcher, or a scientist, because I think it's really super cool.

FUN FACT

A poignant part of my PhD research, which I found an odd comfort in as a disabled woman in research, is that a 'strong' material, isn't always one which can withstand a big load and remain unchanged. A strong, or resilient material, can be one that flexes and deforms, perhaps even cracks, under pressure.

Atoms move, and the structure is changed to absorb the force, and as such, can withstand higher loads. When a material is ductile (able to be deformed without losing toughness; pliable, not brittle) in this way, it also means that when it does fail under pressure, rather than a large explosive bang, with shards of materials scattering and causing additional damage, instead there is a slower decline in the integrity of the structure, meaning the material continues to function in a lesser capacity, giving more time and opportunity for an engineer to fix the problem. Having struggled with mental health, and an unreasonable need to be 'strong' it helps me to remember that, strength isn't about facing every challenge unfazed, and that changing, whether it be your environment, your job, your institution or just by taking time out, isn't a weakness, its merely a way to absorb the pressure to be able to continue functioning, to continue living.

ACTIVITY

A favourite of mine (ironically) is chocolate testing! I think it works particularly well as I am in no danger of eating all the experimental material before gaining results, though you may have more difficulty with that!

Take a look at a range of chocolates, this could be a celebration box of different types, or a few different bars of your choosing. Now, try breaking them in half, squishing them in your fingers, twisting and stretching, and hitting them. Consider the following thoughts:

- Which ones do you think are the 'strongest', and why?

- Do some break as soon as you try to snap them, but don't break when you stretch them?

- Does the whole chocolate bar stay intact, or are there parts that break first?

- What is the chocolate bar made of – caramel, chocolate, biscuit?

- How do you think these materials affect how the chocolate bars behave under pressure?

- You need to make: a rope, a spaceship and a safety helmet, out of the chocolate bars you have. Which chocolate bar would you use for each purpose and why?

The reason behind this exercise is to examine different types of materials, and how they can be strong in different ways. We might look at how they behave under tension (breaking), under shear stress (stretching), under impact (hitting) or under torque (twisting) to help characterise properties such as tensile strength, impact strength and shear strength. In reality, a material may not be strong in all aspects, so we choose the strength we need for a particular purpose. Or perhaps, we try to combine these materials and create a composite (think a chocolate bar with both caramel and biscuit).

One last research question, just for me, which chocolate bar do you think is the tastiest?

LYNDSAY MUIR

Age: 55
Ethnicity: White, British
Gender and sexuality: Female, bisexual
Geographical location: Lincoln, UK
Current institution: Bishop Grosseteste University, UK

ABOUT ME

I am a qualified teacher, a university-based teacher educator, researcher and drama specialist. I'm also a wife, parent and sister. I transitioned later in life, without changing employment, without moving home and with the staunch, enlightened and principled 'wrap around' support of my professional colleagues. I have been gifted with the unflinching, generous affirmation of my loved ones, together with many lifelong and more recent friends, who have walked alongside me on this journey. I am painfully aware of how fortunate I am, yet it would be wrong to imply that it has been easy for anyone, least of all me. It has taken many moons to peel away years of denial and self-loathing, together with the impact of unnecessary, unjustified and unacceptable acts of unkindness (to put it mildly). However, rather than conform to pre-determined and media sanctioned (often distorted and frequently sensationalised) narratives, I embrace the challenges and complexity of gender diversity and non-conformity as enrichment and gift.

FUN FACT

I fulfilled a life-time ambition to perform at the Edinburgh Fringe appearing (albeit briefly!) as a member of the Adam World Choir digital chorus in the National Theatre Scotland's (NTS) award winning, Fringe First production of Adam at the Traverse Theatre, August 2018.

During the global pandemic, the production was adapted for screen and filmed as part of the BBC 'Lights up' (a virtual theatre festival during lockdown), and broadcast on BBC TV – so unexpectedly (and fleetingly!) ending up on the telly!

Adam – written and adapted by Frances Poet and directed by Cora Bissett has just been awarded a Scottish BAFTA (November 2021).

MY RESEARCH

My research is at the intersection of teacher education, trans-studies and drama (or 'applied drama'). I achieved my Master's (Drama in Education) in 1994 and while my comparative study on Bertolt Brecht and Dorothy Heathcote was published under the title 'New Beginnings' in 1996, I took a long and circuitous route back towards research, only finally, after much meandering, registering for my PhD in professional practice at the University of Manchester in 2015. I have always had 'one foot' in education, having qualified as a secondary drama teacher in 1990, so it made sense for me, to research my more recent (and current) professional practice, as a Teacher Educator, supporting, I hope, new generations of secondary drama specialists, in their professional transitions. So it is that I have taken notions, insights and experiences of transitioning from the academic field of trans-studies and used those as a 'trans lens' through which to develop and analyse creative and

critical, drama informed practices to support and enhance the transitioning processes of trainee teachers towards their professional identities as educators. I've given this the title 'A Teacher's Progress – passing as a professional'.

Rather than positioning myself or other gender diverse people as we have been, historically, as problematic, burdensome and delusional, instead I offer a trans-lens as a potential gift and tentative contribution to the research of new knowledge. As Kate Bornstein once stated, everyone has to work

at being themselves, 'transgendered people are probably more aware of doing the work, that's all' (Bornstein, 1995, p. 66).

FUN FACT

Part way through my PhD research I did a TEDx talk entitled 'Tea with Trans: what's on (and off) the menu' (2017).

There's a particularly powerful extract with the Adam World Choir, singing at the end; I'm grateful to all the individual choir members who were able to give their consent for this to be used at the end of my talk, and for NTS enabling this to be done – a global undertaking, and across countries where some people put themselves at risk, for agreeing and participating.

ACTIVITY

Best done with a trusted person but could be done alone.
Think about all that you are, all that you do. Make a list.
Review the list – what do you feel most comfortable with?
When are you, most 'you'?
Bring to mind a moment when you first felt that.

Give yourself two minutes (kitchen timer ideal!): describe the detail, the specifics, set the scene of the exact moment, so that someone else could 'get the picture' from you. (If someone is listening, do just that, listen, no interruptions.) Swap roles.

Now ask, if you had to distil (no gin involved, but does mean concentrate and intensify!) that moment down to its core essentials. It is like a frozen image – only allow yourself a sound, a word or phrase and one gesture if it adds significance.

Now ask these questions of that (autoethnographic; quasi-fictional) moment:

- What is happening?

- Why

- What's at stake?

- Where did you/they learn it from?

- Is this how life should/should not be?

These questions are borrowed from Dorothy Heathcote's five layers of meaning (Davis, 2014; Gillham, 1988; Muir, 1996).

Consider (or discuss with a trusted person) what other moments link with this and what map of your 'progress' through a personal/professional life starts to emerge and how you have/are negotiating that landscape.

LINDA BAINES

Age: Almost 70 in human years; 42 in my head, thinking and approach to life.

Ethnicity: I'm White European. I reject describing myself as British as I am ashamed and embarrassed by what 'UK' has come to stand for, to represent and its narrow-minded hypocrisy. I'm ashamed of the UK government, by its sleaze and corruption, its 'we're here to promote and protect the interests of the rich and the rest of you and the planet can go hang', the running down and removal of compassion for the sick, disabled and vulnerable, of removing essential services and privatising the NHS, of scapegoating others who cannot speak for themselves whose voices and views are ignored and trodden over.

Gender and sexuality: Cis woman

Geographical location: Near Oxford, UK

Current institution: I am an independent researcher and a visiting researcher at University of Southampton, UK. I also volunteer in the third sector as a trustee, chair and mentor.

ABOUT ME

I was brought up in a lower middle-class family on the edges of south Manchester, the eldest of three and the odd one out, and I escaped via university (the first one in the family to go to higher education) via a student grant. I am a lifelong feminist and as I try to grow up, I'm going back to my root political beliefs. I've had low level depression for most of my life

due to childhood experiences. Books have been and continue to be my escape and salvation.

FUN FACT

In 2019, I spent a week in a place that sounds like the colour my hair was as a child.

MY RESEARCH

I became a researcher very late on when my employer sponsored me to undertake a masters and I found the research part the most interesting. I got the bug and started my PhD just before I retired and completed it in 2016. My doctoral research explored the ethical issues and questions which can arise in knowledge exchange, which universities and public sector laboratories undertake and approaches that can be applied to managing them. In the last five years, I've been involved in research on the sharing/gig economy, precarious work, disabled entrepreneurs, women's leadership and I'm now developing a research project focusing on exploring feminist governance and leadership in the third sector. I became a researcher because I'm curious ('nosey') and want to explore, learn and understand phenomena that arise and experiences that people encounter in real life in a practical non-theoretical way. Being a researcher gives me a set of tools and way of working and framework in which I can do this. It also makes me think and question, and gives me a focus and purpose, especially in COVID-19 times where I have a very vulnerable partner and we are constrained in what we can do, where we can go and who we can see.

FUN FACT

My lived experience informs much of my research.

ACTIVITY

Arts-based research methods includes building models as a way to research and understand the world around us because sometimes it's difficult to put things into words and we need to express them or understand them in different ways. We can also see patterns in the similarities or differences between people's models. Explaining the model also helps us to talk about how we think about what we have been asked to create.

Get different coloured packs of Playdoh or similar material, or Lego. You can use these materials to construct a model of how you understand a phenomenon such as leadership (my research area) but you can use this method to explore yours and other people's understandings of lots of different things and not just leadership.

SOPHIA COOKE

Age: 30
Ethnicity: White British
Gender and sexuality: Woman, heterosexual
Geographical location: Galápagos Islands
Current institution: University of Cambridge, UK

ABOUT ME

On the outside I look like I have it all together. I appear confident, fun, energetic and happy. But I suffer deeply with anxiety and, since an abusive relationship a few years ago, post-traumatic stress disorder. Every day is a battle with fear, and this affects every aspect of my work and my personal life. I struggle in my relationships with friends and colleagues, and I exhaust myself daily. My work, however, never ignites fear in me but passion, excitement and drive. I love what I do and it helps me to muffle those inner voices.

FUN FACT

I have always struggled to slow my mind down – it jumps from thought to thought. When I was 13, I was given my first camera and set about photographing everything I came across – wildlife, people and objects. To my delight, I discovered mental peace for the first time. When I look down my lens, I think of nothing but what I can see. Now the walls of

my home are full of photos I have taken and every single one makes me smile.

MY RESEARCH

I have always had a love of understanding the world, asking questions and finding the answers. The natural world runs through my core and one of the questions I continually return to is what our place, as humans, is in it. So, although I did not know I wanted to work in conservation and sustainability when I went to university, having found myself here makes perfect sense. My dream is for people to be able to live alongside nature, in sync with their environment, and to be protectors of it. For this, they need to be protected too. So, we need to eradicate poverty, achieve gender equality, reduce waste and ensure everyone has access to good education. That is why I now work to aid the achievement of the United Nations Sustainable Development Goals (UN SDGs) in Galápagos. If we can achieve true sustainability and equality here, I believe these magical islands can set an example to the world, and give what we need most of right now – hope.

FUN FACT

Every day I do something different – educate young people, plant trees, swim with sealions, interview fishermen, write articles, do bird surveys and build software. I wake up every morning and decide what I want to do that day. Sometimes I feel I need 100 of me but I am never bored!

ACTIVITY

There are 17 UN SDGs adopted by all United Nations Member States in 2015. You can find out more via this website https://sdgs.un.org/goals

The goals are a blueprint for peace and prosperity for now and our future. These goals are concerned with how reducing poverty, improving education and the economy go hand in hand with tackling climate change and preserving our planet.

In groups, choose and research one SDG and then teach the other groups about it. You can be creative in the way you teach about the SDG such as doing a speech, a lesson, a poster or even a short film.

ADELE PAVLIDIS

Age: 41
Ethnicity: I was born in Australia to European migrants (father from Malta, mother from Greece).
Gender and sexuality: I am a woman, married to a man, I am also a mother of two boys.
Geographical location: Gold Coast, Australia

ABOUT ME

I grew up in Melbourne, in an extremely diverse area. For primary school the majority of students were Vietnamese migrants and refugees (in 1980s) and I grew up in a very multicultural community. My father was a small business person and so I grew up in video and record shops, pool halls and restaurants. It was a fun childhood but also I had to grow up fast. I always loved school and went to an all-girls high school. For a number of reasons, I ended up leaving home and dropping out of school before finishing. I was 16 and living with my boyfriend. This relationship became violent and I was lucky to survive his abuse and threats. I eventually left Melbourne and re-established myself in another state where I went to TAFE (vocational education) to gain entry to university. I enrolled in a BA and fell in love with sociology. Turned out I was great at it! Since then, I have worked as a youth worker, drug and alcohol worker and then eventually as an academic. I research sport and leisure, with a particular

focus on roller sports! I am passionate about gender equity and supporting women to be kick ass versions of themselves! I now have two sons who I am raising to be feminists.

FUN FACT

I did my PhD about roller derby and conducted an ethnographic study. An ethnography is where you observe and study a human culture. To observe the culture of roller derby I had to learn to skate and eventually learnt to jump over a person! Yew! I am now learning to skate jam (dancing) which I am loving.

MY RESEARCH

I research the gendered power relations in sport and leisure. This includes feelings of inclusion and exclusion, wellbeing and organisational micropolitics. I am interested in the ways we think about change – how does a person change? How does a culture change? These are the questions that drive me. I have situated my research in sport and leisure contexts as I believe they are so important – having interests and capabilities outside of work! Learning to leisure is hard! Alcohol and drug consumption is easy (and can cause issues) but other leisure practices can take work and time and navigation.

I have published two books (with one on the way) and over 40 peer-reviewed articles/book chapters on these topics.

FUN FACT

Lots of interesting/fun facts. I travelled to China to meet with the local derby league and found the influence of feminist ideas flowing through the sport. I have also created new methodologies, including a time capsule methodology, where teenage

girls were asked to communicate with the future about their experience of COVID-19. I even write poetry as a way to express research findings and emphasise emotion and affects!

ACTIVITY

Poetry and research and sport

This is an activity to get you thinking about how a person might shift from 'bad feelings' to 'good ones'.

1. Find a sport or activity you haven't done much of (I recommend roller skating, skate boarding, surfing, rock climbing, but even weightlifting or boxing!) and safely organise to try it out.

2. After your first try, experiment with writing a poem that expresses how you felt.

3. Share this poem with others (whoever you feel safe with) and encourage them to try the activity too.

4. Reflect together on how leisure and sport can support wellbeing. Also, what are the problems with sport and leisure?

ALLISON UPSHAW

Age: 54
Ethnicity: African American
Gender and sexuality: Heterosexual
Geographical location: Alabama, USA
Current institution: Stillman College, USA (a HBCU, Historically Black College and Universities)

ABOUT ME

I am a world traveller from a rural background. My grandmother only received a third-grade education, while my mother went on to graduate with a master's degree in education. I am the product of a single parent home as my father died before I was born. My arts background (I am a trained opera singer and professional actress) and interdisciplinary approach to research combined with my perspective as a US African American brings forth a wealth of diversity in my work.

FUN FACT

I'm a professionally trained opera singer who used to perform poetry for a living. I am also on a mission to drive in every single state in the United States. I only have 7 left!

MY RESEARCH

I explore the storied lives of US African American rural women. I braid artistic layers of inquiry and practice into critical performative ethnographies. It seems I've always been a story-teller (story singer maybe), and gaining my doctorate just honed that skill. My work rarely begins with a research question, rather it begins with a puzzle that I just can't quite solve. The drive to fit the pieces together makes me a researcher.

FUN FACT

I created my own method, L'OPERA: Layered Operations Practicing Embodiment, Reflection and Analysis. I braid artistic inquiry through music, dance, theatre and visual art to tell culturally relevant stories of African American women.

ACTIVITY

My current puzzle revolves around the United States, African American female landowners from the end of the Civil War until the present day. I'd like to use an Adinkra card set to visually reflect themes that I find through interviews and archival records. Using the cards to facilitate discussions with family members and with my own perspectives of the data that I mine from my sources, I also plan to incorporate them into a newly created visual analysis or reflection of my work.

Adinkra symbols originate from West Africa. They link West African History with spiritualism. The cards can be used in various ways and have been used in clinical psychology. You can find images of Adinkra symbols online (see some

examples below) or even buy sets of the cards. You could interview your own family or friends on a topic of your choosing and then use the symbols where you see each theme come up in the interview. This will give you a picture/symbol representation of the interview to help you see the themes in people's life stories. What would your life story look like in Adinkra symbols?

ADINKRA SYMBOLS

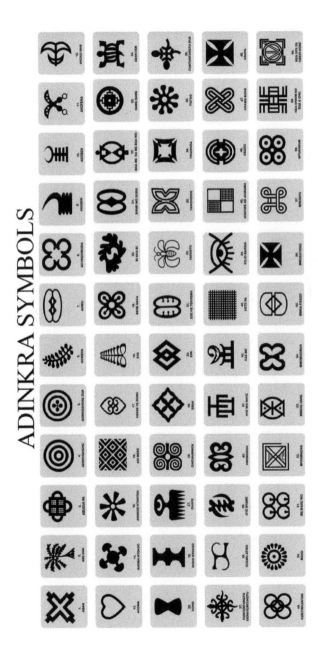

HELEN ROSS

Age: 40
Ethnicity: I'm white and British. I grew up in England.
Gender and sexuality: I'm cisgender female – married with a little boy.
Geographical location: South West England – near Bath in a little town called Trowbridge.

ABOUT ME

My background is very privileged, but not always straight-forward. I found out I was dyslexic when I was 17 and that explained a whole lot of feelings: I've never felt clever enough or good enough (that continues now!).

I did mechanical engineering and French at university; first time round and I was going to be a chartered engineer by the age of 30.

Spoiler alert: I am not an engineer.

I worked in engineering and had, 'You're a girl? What are you doing this job for?' implied, without those words ever being used. I crashed into depression and anxiety, then became a teacher.

Barnsley and the pit villages changed my soul. My dyslexia became the fire in my belly to make me better for our children. I've worked with children with Special Educational Needs for 15 years now and the more I see of them, the more I see of me.

Dyslexia and other quirks – I am 99% sure I have attention deficit hyperactivity disorder (ADHD) – underpin everything I do and how I do it. I have a goldfish brain; I write EVERYTHING down. My organisation would be awful if I didn't have a phone to shout at me when I need to do 'stuff' and reading is the bane of my life. I have to do it so I do, but it takes everything in me to manage to read articles without text-to-speech.

I'm quirky and I make a HUGE noise about it, hopefully benefitting others who can't make as much noise.

FUN FACT

I love to travel and learn different languages. The main reason I started to learn different languages is because I am so ridiculously nosy. I hated that I couldn't understand what was happening around me when I used to visit my Dad in France, when I was 15. So, I decided that I'd start to learn and discovered a whole new world of culture, and experience and loved it. I like playing out on my bike and hurtle around Wiltshire like a wally whenever I can – it is just good for the soul to have the wind between my ears!

MY RESEARCH

Most of my research is based around Special Educational Needs, focusing particularly on dyslexia, literacy and specific learning difficulties. I explore lived experiences of young people, their teachers and their families through an emancipatory lens (where participants have freedom of expression). I use work inspired by the French sociologist Pierre Bourdieu who writes about how power shapes our cultures and us as individuals. I have developed his ideas for my own work.

I am dyslexic and struggle to read – I can but I don't like it. As a teacher, working with young people who find literacy and engagement with learning challenging, I became thoroughly disenfranchised with governmental diktats landing in my inbox that had so  little relevance to the children I was teaching and the world I was working in. When I looked at consultations, there was so much reference to people based in universities and/or with PhDs so I decided I need to work for, and earn one, so that I could start to make contributions to consultations, literature and, ultimately, government policy. I am so fortunate that I now get to do that.

I also continue to work in school for two days a week as a Special Educational Needs (SEN) teacher, as well as being a dyslexia/SpLD assessor – for me, the research and the lived experience are totally intertwined and I can't imagine researching teaching, SEN and not working in it as a practitioner. It is my calling and I am very lucky to be able to work, consult and research in something that is so close to my heart.

FUN FACT

My research, in fact all of my work around Special educational needs and disabilities (SEND) and inclusion is borne out of rage, anger and general strop. I have dyslexia and I spent many years in school feeling completely inadequate. I do not want any other children or young people (or anyone actually) to feel like that. This history, combined with a few years teaching in a tricky area where government policy just seemed totally irrelevant, or out of touch at best, put the fire in my belly to learn how to do policy stuff. So, I did a PhD.

ACTIVITY

Match celebrities to their neurodiversity, then ask participants to define those neurodiversities.

Neurodiversity is where we process information and understand the world in non-typical ways. This includes ADHD, attention deficit disorder (ADD), autism, dyslexia, dyscalculia, obsessional compulsive disorder, oppositional defiance disorder, dyspraxia, etc.

You may have heard of or, indeed, be neurodiverse. It is inevitable that many celebrities or famous people in areas, such as sport, entertainment, etc., will also be neurodiverse.

Find some examples of famous neurodiverse people. Next, link the formal definitions of those diversities to the person. Finally reflect on or note down how the definition matches your understanding of that famous persons celebrity profiles. Did you have any previous misconceptions about neurodiverse people that has now been challenged by finding examples within the world of celebrity?

IMPLICATIONS AND APPLICATION OF FINDINGS

In exploring people's conception of neurodiversity and linking them to influential people, you can be empowered to understand and embrace differences as well as appreciate how difference adds richness to our lives.

GEMMA MASSON

Age: 33
Ethnicity: White British
Gender and sexuality: Female pansexual
Geographical location: Birmingham, UK
Current institution: University of Birmingham, UK

ABOUT ME

I am from a working-class background and have self-funded my education with jobs since I was 16. I won't lie that having to work as well as study at the same time was a strain and may have impacted my studies, but ever since I was 11 and found out what a PhD was, I was determined to have one. As a lifelong bookworm and learner, the idea that I could learn and study as an occupation was irresistible! My family was not able or willing to support my studies either financially or emotionally as they see very little purpose in academia so as I said, I self-supported most of my studies, with the exception of small study grants. Additionally, I suffer from chronic stress and anxiety for which I have had therapy and am still medicated and supervised. My mental health issues primarily come from a broken home and abusive childhood and came to a head at the end of my PhD studies. It was a perfect storm of stress and long-term post-traumatic stress disorder, which finally broke the camel's back and I had to apply for an extension on my studies, which made me feel worse, ironically!

However, I am now doing much better (there is no 'cure' for chronic mental health), but I am finally properly managing my conditions. Finally, my sexuality. Despite being in a monogamous marriage to a cis-male I am pansexual but often find it hard to express this or find acceptance.

FUN FACT

From age 27 onwards I became very interested in health and fitness, participating in multiple group exercise classes at my gym (my favourites are Zumba, Barre, Cycle and Combat!) I am now a licensed Zumba Instructor and studying for my Exercise to Music Diploma.

This is my way of dealing with my negative body image issues and mental health issues surrounding my body and food. I also want to encourage love of health and bodies in others which is why Zumba is such a good fit for me, although I do plan to qualify in several other programmes as well.

MY RESEARCH

I read both recreationally as well as professionally! My love of stories and natural inclination towards the humanities led me to take both English Literature and History at A-Level in school. However, I found that the stories I read for pleasure often led to me to look into their real-world context and so settled onto history for my university study. I was also concerned that if I became too involved in dissecting literature it would stop being a pleasure to read and I would lose the escapism. Furthermore, I enjoy creative writing for pleasure and felt vindicated in my choice not to pursue this at university from a friend who did and found the process unrewarding and disillusioning. In this way, I managed to maintain the joy I find in consuming and creating stories while

pursuing my love of them through history. Also, I maintain if you are going to love stories, there is no larger story than history to dive into – there is always more of it to explore and discover!

It was my love of read-ing which brought me to the field of Ottoman stud-ies. I read The Historian by Elizabeth Kostova during the summer break between my BA and MA and found myself instantly obsessed! This led to an independ-ent study and MA thesis based around the Ottoman  Empire during my MA before I explored PhD options in this field. I came to Birmingham as a PhD student in this area and completed my thesis on *The Urban Janissary in Eighteenth Century Istanbul.*

FUN FACT

My aim was to overturn historical stereotypes of this type of military group and to debunk the 'decline' of the institution, framing it instead as an institutional transformation based on the changing context of the eighteenth century world. Istan-bul, as the Ottoman capital, was at the centre of these changes and also provided the most archival evidence for this study. Hence my choice to focus on the city. I also had the chance to study an imperial capital as a region instead of being consid-ered indicative of the entirety of a very diverse empire. There are also several interesting historical parallels to be assessed including the Knights Templar, Praetorian Guard, Egyptian Mamluks, among others.

ACTIVITY

Outside of specialist courses on Islamic and Eastern studies which must be deliberately sought out many students in the UK are not aware of the existence of the Ottomans. For this reason, many students can be put off or discouraged from pursuing wider areas of history, preferring to stay to the familiar areas they have been taught at school that they are comfortable with.

This activity can be used in a workshop session or as an ice-breaker. This activity not only introduces key figures and circumstances in Ottoman history but also encourages you to put yourself into the minds and perspectives of historical characters, which teaches the importance of contextualising history.

The activity is a 'What Would You Do?'

Research a scenario from Ottoman history which features at least one important historical figure.

Re-write the scenario and think what would you do in this situation? For example, you are a young prince in the early fifteenth century, your father has abdicated but the advisers don't trust you, what would you do?

You can work individually or in groups to discuss the problem. Bonus kudos points if anyone else participating can guess who the historical figure may be.

LAUREN ALEX O'HAGAN

Age: 30
Ethnicity: White European (British/Irish)
Gender and sexuality: Female, heterosexual
Geographical location: Örebro, Sweden
Current institution: Örebro University, Sweden

ABOUT ME

I grew up in a working-class family in a poor, culturally diverse area of Bristol, England. My academic journey has been a constant struggle in the face of social class barriers, yet, through hard work and perseverance, I have been able to achieve my goals. I wanted to pursue a career as a translator, but there were limited subject options at my school, so I spent my free time teaching myself French, Spanish and Italian. I managed to obtain A Level in all three subjects, receiving the highest result in the UK for Italian and receiving a letter of recognition from the Italian Consulate. After leaving college, I undertook a degree with the Open University, working full-time to support myself. I then progressed to MA and PhD, during which time I set up my own translation and proof-reading business to fund my studies.

Another major struggle throughout my life is my mental health. At 14 years old, I was diagnosed with an anxiety and panic disorder, which makes day-to-day life very challenging. Tasks or social situations that may seem normal for most

people are an uphill battle for me. I have received very little support for my condition and have only started to tell others about it in recent years to break the stigma and show that mental illness does not have to define you and that EVERY-BODY is capable of achieving great things.

If you've got a dream, then chase it!

FUN FACT

My biggest passion is music. I play bass guitar and run an Instagram fanpage and blog for my favourite musician, Rory Gallagher. It is through Rory – who suffered from anxiety and depression throughout his life – that I have found the confidence to talk openly about my own mental health struggles. I use the fanpage and blog to promote his musical legacy, but also to raise general awareness of mental health. I also regularly collaborate with Heavy Metal Therapy, an organisation that uses rock/metal to help mental wellbeing.

Through my advocacy work, I have connected with the Gallagher family and Rory's closest friends.

MY RESEARCH

I was always interested in foreign languages and, from a young age, wanted to be a translator. I studied English, Spanish and Italian at university and, at the same time, worked in (and later managed) a second-hand bookshop, where I developed a knowledge of antiquarian books and became interested in the ownership marks left inside. I had planned to undertake an MA in Translation, but towards the end of my degree, I came across a piece of research that changed my life: it was a study by Prof. Julia Gillen on Edwardian postcards and what their images and text could tell us about life in early twentieth century Britain. Reading her work, I suddenly realised that

I could combine my love for books, history and languages into one career path as a researcher in Sociolinguistics. I swiftly changed my plans and studied MA in Applied Linguistics, followed by PhD in Language and Communication, specialising in performances of social class in Edwardian book inscriptions. In 2021,  I wrote a monograph on the topic, which was published with Routledge. I have since developed this research further by looking more broadly at class relations and material culture in the Edwardian era, covering food advertisements, propaganda postcards and writing implements. In the last three years, I have also developed a secondary – and very different – research area of Irish musicology, where I investigate expressions of Irish identity in popular song lyrics, music videos and YouTube comments.

FUN FACT

Through my book inscription research, I have uncovered the hidden histories of more than 1,500 working-class Edwardians. I have found that working-class inscribers used the spaces in their books not just to mark ownership, but also as diary entries to record personal events in their lives, challenge established religion and show support for socialism and women's suffrage. Their marks, therefore, offer new perspectives on working-class life, contesting stereotypes around illiteracy or lack of intelligence and demonstrating that many people were, in fact, politically active, well-educated and able

to oppose their marginalised status through the power of writing.

ACTIVITY

Look around your home for old books or talk to your family and friends and see what old books they might have. Start flipping through them for annotations, scribbles, doodles or any other signs of ownership. Look particularly on the front and back inside covers – a spot where many people choose to inscribe. Do you know the owner? If yes, what do you know about them? Are any of the things you know about them reflected in their inscription? If you don't know the owner, think about where you could go to find out more information about him/her. Why not visit your local library, where you can access www.ancestry.com, a database full of historical records like census returns, military papers and birth, marriage and death certificates? Use the information in the inscription (e.g. name, date and geographical location) to try and track down the person. Are there any clues about their social class from the census? What about the inscription itself (e.g. handwriting, spelling and grammar) or the book in which it is written? Do you think inscriptions are a valuable tool to learn about the past? What else might be learnt from them?

JESSICA KORTE

Age: 31
Ethnicity: Caucasian
Gender and sexuality: Probably female, possibly non-binary. Queer/bisexual
Geographical location: Australia
Current institution: University of Queensland, Australia

ABOUT ME

I am a queer woman in STEM (specifically IT) (although I am currently questioning my gender identity and exploring non-binary gender). I am an early career researcher (PhD awarded in 2017).

I am passionate about the ways good technology can improve lives. To ensure technology is 'good', I advocate involving end users in design processes. My philosophy for technology design is that the needs of people who are disempowered or disabled by society should be considered first; everyone else will then benefit from technology that maximises usability. This philosophy holds true in my TASDCRC Fellowship Project, the Auslan Communication Technologies Pipeline project, which looks to foreground the visual-gestural language expertise of Deaf signers in the creation of technologies for the recognition, production and processing of Auslan (Australian Sign Language) communication.

FUN FACT

I'm a superhero! Well, sort of.

I wrote the short story 'IF' in the first Tech Girls are Super-heroes book. While the story isn't about me, the character is modelled on me:

MY RESEARCH

I research participatory design with deaf people. In my PhD research I developed YoungDeafDesign, a participatory design method for designing technology with and for deaf children aged three to five, with the intention that it could be used to create better educational technologies. My current research project involves designing a digital personal assistant

(like an Alexa, Siri or Google Home) which understands and responds to Auslan, the sign language of the Australian Deaf community.

I became a researcher, and specifically a technology design researcher, because I recognise that good technologies can improve lives – but only if they are well-designed, considering the needs and abilities of all users.

FUN FACT

Young deaf kids are incredibly creative communicators! During my PhD, I worked with three- to five-year-old deaf kids who have hearing parents. They were still learning their first languages: Auslan, Australia's sign language, and one or more spoken languages, usually what their parents speak. I was also learning Auslan, and was about as good as the kids. Despite that we worked together for most of a year, doing activities to help me learn about the children's abilities and interests. The children would communicate in a mix of signing, miming and vocalisations.

ACTIVITY

How do technology designers make technologies better?

Think about an app, programme or website you use often that has an annoying problem (e.g. Does an activity take too many steps?, Is it hard to find things you're looking for? and Do you see content that isn't interesting?)

On some sticky notes, write down:

- Three things you like.

- Three things you dislike.

- Three ways it could be improved. (These can address the 'what you don't like', but they can also be different.)

Ask some friends/family members who also use the app/programme/website to do this too, until you have a little collection of data. On a large surface, sort the sticky notes into groups. There are many ways of doing this, but some suggestions are:

- If multiple people like/dislike/would improve the same thing, group those notes together.

- Group dislikes with improvements that would fix them.

- Look for dislikes which don't have suggested improvements.

- Look for suggested improvements which don't match with dislikes; or which would break something someone else likes.

This type of activity lets designers know what is good, bad and how to improve technologies they're working on. It isn't always easy – sometimes people disagree about what is good or bad in a technology; sometimes fixing one problem will introduce a new one. But it is always important to ask the people who are using a technology what their experience is like – that is the only way to make sure you're solving real problems, and not breaking things which are working.

JULIETTE WILSON-THOMAS

Age: 37
Ethnicity: White of mixed English/Irish heritage
Gender and sexuality: Woman in a heterosexual relationship.
Geographical location: Manchester, UK
Current institution: Manchester Metropolitan University, UK

ABOUT ME

My parents had me when they were young and studying at university. My mum dropped out to care for me, and then my two brothers, but went back to university to study teaching and graduated as a mature student. I was part of my parents' higher education journey and they were first generation students. I then also had my children while I was young and completed all of my postgraduate studies while caring for my two small children and working. First I undertook a teaching English course, partially via distance learning, at Sheffield Hallam University, and then I studied for online postgraduate qualifications with the Open University (OU) in social sciences and child development. I was also employed as a family support worker for a family centre during this period.

When I completed my OU studies the culmination was a research proposal which we were encouraged to use for further study, that is, a PhD, which I had never considered as something for someone like me before. I only applied to a

funded teaching studentship at Salford University, as I would not have been able to afford an unfunded one, and was successful in being accepted as a graduate teaching assistant on a PhD programme sociology course at Salford University. My daughter was three years and son was one year when I embarked on my PhD, and I completed my studies in three years (because that was all that was funded!), while teaching, commuting and caring.

FUN FACT

When I started my PhD I did not believe that I would finish because it was not a world I knew much about, and I did not really believe I was capable of it. However, the stipend was more than I would earn after paying for childcare in the jobs I had been working, and I was able to pay for less childcare by working at the weekends and at night, so I didn't think I had anything to lose! I surprised myself by getting halfway through successfully, and then just kept going.

MY RESEARCH

I'm a sociological researcher interested in inequality and policy responses to inequality. From my personal and professional background, I experienced many contexts of inequality and I wanted to understand more about why they occur and what can be done to make positive changes. In 2008, I was working as a family support worker and the financial crash happened, which meant that much of the work for preventative services was cut or reduced. I became a researcher to provide deeper answers to why important work which helps people would be stopped, and what could be done to reduce inequality in a more sustained way.

I was also particularly interested in the experiences of young mothers as I was one, and worked with many, and understood some of the gendered inequities faced when raising children in our society.

In my research I came across alternative economic practices, for example, creating new forms of money, and thought that different ways to value people's time and efforts were a good way to do something about inequality. I thought that these practices would be particularly useful for women with children who are often unable to gain meaningful and rewarding paid work, but who also do so much work for society which deserves compensation. I chose to research time banks which are an alternative economic group who create money based on time; one hour's work, for one time credit. For example, a member may teach an hour's English lesson to another member and receive one time credit which they can use to pay for an hour's gardening from another member. I researched time banks to understand the different ways we could better value the undervalued work in society.

FUN FACT

Alternative economic practices are relatively minor activities, but any challenge to money is taken quite seriously by those in power. While I was researching time banks The Bank of England released a statement about the extent that such practices would be tolerated within our economy, and they stated that alternative currencies would be addressed if they started to challenge mainstream money. This is quite funny really, given that alternative currency groups are all very small and marginal activities, but it does demonstrate how seriously government institutions take any challenge to their power over money.

ACTIVITY

Develop a list of all the activities your mother/parent/guardian does for you in a day and try to find the market value for each of these activities and add it up. For example, waking you up? In hotels they charge for this. Making your breakfast? What premium do you pay in a restaurant for someone to make your food? Washing your clothes, what would a laundrette charge? Loving you? Can we quantify this?

Try to come up with a wage for all these services and consider if and how the government could fund this. You could consider the wages paid to foster parents as a way into this.

This activity would raise all kinds of questions about work, value, society, gender, emotional labour, etc. Should these activities be done for free? Or do they have value to the rest of society, and should those who perform these activities be disadvantaged by performing them for no pay? What strategies do you think the government could implement to properly value this work? You could create your own currency and compensation policy to address this.

KATE MASSEY-CHASE

Age: 34
Ethnicity: White British
Gender and sexuality: Woman/female, using she/her pronouns.
Queer/bisexual
Geographical location: Exeter, Devon, UK
Current institution: Plymouth Marjon University, UK

ABOUT ME

I'm a queer woman in my 30s. I live in Devon (UK) with my
wife, our little baby and our two cats. I work part-time at
Plymouth Marjon University as a Lecturer in the Performing Arts Department, where I've just designed a new MA in
Arts, Health and Wellbeing (the rest of the time, I do hourly
paid work as a Careers Advisor at the University of Exeter –
or play with our baby!). The topic of arts and health is important to me. When I was a teenager, I really struggled and
became very unwell, even spending some time in hospital. I
started to get a bit better when I went to university, although
it's taken many years. What really helped was the chance to
pursue my passion for theatre in a supportive environment.
I started to learn about ways I could use creative practices
to support others, which was really inspiring and gave me
a sense of purpose. I then did my Masters in 'Applied Theatre', which was about using drama in the community, and I
worked freelance after that, running workshops in addiction

recovery services, mental health services, with young refugees and lots of other groups. I wrote about some of this work for my PhD. I think my experiences of mental illness have made me more empathetic. And empathy is a powerful force. When I face challenges now, I also have lots of coping strategies, self-knowledge and inner strength to draw from.

FUN FACT

When I was 14 years, my mum took me to see West Side Story in Winchester Prison, performed by a cast of prisoners and professional actors. It was such an inspiring experience and opened my eyes to the amazing possibilities for using the arts for personal  and social change. Six years later, I was in my first prison theatre production (in the same prison). I later went on to co-edit a book about theatre in prisons; one of the chapters, called 'From the Fishbowl to the Sea', was written by a prisoner who'd been in one of the plays.

MY RESEARCH

I research how socially engaged theatre practices (sometimes called 'applied theatre') can be used for personal, social and political purposes. My PhD – which I was awarded in 2021 – explores how applied theatre could support young people in the transition between Child & Adolescent and Adult Mental Health Services. People who had experienced this transition, their parents/carers and the professionals who work with them told me about how it felt, and then I used my professional experience of using drama in the community, and the experience of other practitioners and academics, to consider

ways that theatre-based practices might be able to make this transition better. I also drew on my own experiences of being a mental health service user, using a methodology called 'autoethnography'. This means that you also belong to the group you are studying and you include your own experiences in your research. I felt a bit nervous about doing this, but ultimately, it's made my research more powerful.

I moved into doing research when I started my PhD, when I was 28 years old, after working freelance for five years. I really enjoyed my work in the community, but I was also tired of juggling multiple jobs on insecure contracts and wanted to start a family. I knew academia wasn't an easy career path, but I was determined and had my heart set on becoming a lecturer. This job has meant that I can teach, which I love, as well as doing my own research.

FUN FACT

Have you ever thought about how when you go to the doctor and they ask you questions, they are prompting a form of storytelling? Feminist philosopher, Pyne Addelson coined the term 'cognitive authority' to mean that your descriptions of the world are taken seriously and believed. My research showed how young mental health service users aren't always taken seriously and believed when they tell the stories of their experiences in treatment settings. They can feel stigmatised, because they are young and unwell, and it can make them feel powerless and like they are losing control of their own story.

ACTIVITY

Draw a quick picture of yourself, head to toe. This could be just an outline, like a cookie cutter or you can make it more detailed if you enjoy drawing.

Next, take a moment to look down at your own body, maybe starting with your hands, then your arms, thinking about your face, your height and your hair. What memories and stories spring to mind? Here are some of mine:

- I have a scar on my left arm from falling out of a tree when I was seven years.

- I have short hair because I cut it myself with kitchen scissors when I was little and kept it that way to look different from my twin sister.

- I pick at the skin around my nails when I am bored or stressed.

Make notes on your drawing of these stories in the place on your body that makes sense to you. You don't need to go any deeper or more personal than feels comfortable. Take care of yourself; if something brings up a troubling memory, do speak to someone you trust about it. Keep making these notes (and expand on them as much as you wish) until you have as many stories as you can think of. What a rich source of 'data' our bodies can be!

You might like to do this activity with a few friends and then share some of your stories, in as much detail as you like; I'm sure you'll learn things about them you never knew before.

JACKIE CARTER

Age: 61
Ethnicity: British
Gender and sexuality: Woman
Geographical location: Northwest of England, UK
Current institution: University of Manchester, UK

ABOUT ME

I was the first in my family to go to university. My dad worked in a factory, my mum was a dinner lady. I'm one of six kids; I'm number 4. The eldest three all left school at 16. I grew up in Leeds, went to state schools and had a Saturday job as soon as I could (think I was 14) as I liked nice clothes and going out.

I was encouraged by my teachers to stay on into sixth form. I was good at English and Latin (!) at school but I chose Physics, Chemistry and Maths for my A-level as I'd read a book about drug taking and thought I wanted to be a pharmacologist. To be honest I didn't have much of a clue about anything back then and had never even met a scientist. My eldest sister had married a sociology graduate though and they helped me apply to university.

I found a university course that sounded good – it combined Social Psychology with Maths. I started it but had no confidence and didn't do well so I dropped out, worked in a pub for the rest of that year, and then went to do a different

course the following year. I graduated three years later with a degree in Mathematics with its applications. That was such an enormously proud moment and my mum and dad were so pleased. It also set me up for the career I have followed since graduating.

FUN FACT

My family and friends describe me as a bit of a scatterbrain. I think it's because I have so many ideas and my mind is always buzzing, but it means that I end up doing silly things. I once reported my car as stolen, got the police involved and everything. I called home to let them know what had happened and my husband told me that I hadn't taken the car to the shops and it was outside our house. Things like this seem to happen to me a lot, but we have a good laugh about them afterwards.

MY RESEARCH

I research 'social mobility', which examines how people can move from the group they were born in, into other groups during their lives, focusing on how education and work experience affects this. You've seen that my parents were manual workers who left school early, as did three of my siblings. My chances in life changed because I went to university and now that I am a professor, I try to be the person in my students' lives that I wish I'd had when I was their age.

I haven't always worked in a university. My first career was as a Maths teacher in a comprehensive school. I really love teaching – I've got a national award for it – and enjoy helping students learn. I retrained (as a single parent, in my 30s) and got a Master's then a PhD (qualifications you can get after your first degree).

I worked for 14 years *with* academics but not *as* one. Then I started to write about my work and gave presentations on the importance of work experience in opening doors to future careers, especially those students from less-advantaged and underrepresented groups. I won a

million-pound grant to set up a paid work placement scheme and became an academic in my 50s. I have since placed 300 students into paid internships and this informs my research. In 2021 my book *Work Placements, Internships and Applied Social Research* was published. My research is now being used in Colombia and Brazil.

FUN FACT

A university education alone does not open access to a graduate career. My research is opening a diverse talent pipeline to graduate careers that need data-skilled people, by providing work experience during the degree.

My research has created opportunities that give students the chance to practise their skills in the workplace and get paid while doing so. Since 2014 I have placed 300 social science students into paid internships. They have undertaken projects in government departments, charities, universities, think-tanks, research consultancies and banks, working with data and applying their classroom skills in these organisations. Twenty-five per cent are from underrepresented groups or less-advantaged backgrounds and 70 per cent are female.

ACTIVITY

Researching the Area You Study in

This activity will help you explore data through using a database. You will use an interactive map to look at census data that have been collected by the Office for National Statistics (ONS) in the UK. The aim is to explore data repositories/data bases. There are lots of these types of data base for many different types of data. The UK ONS was chosen as a good example where you can access information to explore the patterns of educational outcome (i.e. qualifications). If you are in the UK you can try using your own postcode. If you live outside the UK you can compare these two postcodes from the area of Stockport. Stockport was chosen as it had both high levels of wealth and depravation.

Postcode 1: SK8 7JY.

Postcode 2: SK5 8HH.

We will investigate the questions:

1. What is the highest level of qualification in the area?

2. Which areas close by have higher and lower levels than where I study?

3. What other factors might we explore alongside educational qualifications?

A. Go to the website: datashine.org.uk

B. Enter the postcode of the school where you study and click Go – the map will update to show you the location and surroundings.

C. As we're interested in educational qualifications, we
    need to select the right data to show on the map. In the
    Data Chooser tool (top right) click on Education. Now
    select 'Highest level of qualification' in the first drop-
    down menu and 'Level 4 qualifications and above' in the
    second drop-down menu.

D. Interpret the findings. You need to know what 'Level 4
    qualifications are' – research this definition. Look at the
    pattern on the resulting map and think about what it
    tells you. Write down what you have discovered. There
    is no right or wrong answer.

E. Explore and investigate further. Try changing the second
    drop-down menu and see how the map changes. What
    does this tell you? Now change the first drop-down
    menu and see how the second drop-down menu changes
    too.

F. Think like a researcher. When you explain your results
    think about what other factors you would like to
    explore in addition to educational outcome. Write these
    ideas down.

That's it – you have done some research on educational
differences. Well done.

W0010430